Guerber Hélène Adeline

Legends of the Virgin and Christ

With Special References to Literature and Art

Guerber Hélène Adeline

Legends of the Virgin and Christ
With Special References to Literature and Art

ISBN/EAN: 9783337155407

Printed in Europe, USA, Canada, Australia, Japan

Cover: Foto ©Lupo / pixelio.de

More available books at **www.hansebooks.com**

LEGENDS

OF

THE VIRGIN AND CHRIST

WITH SPECIAL REFERENCE TO
LITERATURE AND ART

BY

H. A. GUERBER

AUTHOR OF "MYTHS OF GREECE AND ROME," "MYTHS OF
NORTHERN LANDS," "CONTES ET LÉGENDES,"
"STORIES OF THE WAGNER OPERA," ETC.

WITH ILLUSTRATIONS

NEW YORK
DODD, MEAD AND COMPANY
1896

AFFECTIONATELY DEDICATED

TO

My Uncle and Aunt,

MR. AND MRS. ADOLPHE L. GUERBER.

PREFACE.

IN visiting the art galleries at home or abroad, or in turning over the pages of the current magazines, we find countless pictures of Christ and the Virgin Mary. Some of the most famous paintings in the world are based upon, or give some hint of, the numerous legends concerning Mother and Son which were so very popular during the Middle Ages.

The prevalence of these tales, only some of which are embodied in the canon of any Christian church, was owing to the fact that they satisfied the childlike curiosity of people anxious to know more about the subject than could be found in the brief but authentic Scriptural account.

Gradually woven into poetry and song, these sacred legends became one of the principal themes of all wandering minstrels, who told them in castle and cot. For many centuries also they formed part of all the dramatic representations, and finally they were seized upon by great artists and transferred to canvas, where they still glow in undimmed beauty, and, in many cases, serve to keep alive traditions which would else have been forgotten.

All those who have grown up in Roman Catholic countries or homes are, of course, more or less familiar with some of the legends related here, which are nearly unknown to the average Protestant reader. While some of them are puerile in the extreme, and even at times childishly and unintentionally sacrilegious, the majority are as beautiful and poetical as untrue.

The aim of this work is not to give a long list of noted pictures, but rather to place before the reader the many legends which have been used for illustration in art or literature. Then, with a distinct idea in his mind, not only of the Scriptural, but also of the legendary lore concerning Christ and the Virgin, it will be easy to trace out the story as told in art, and to gain a clearer insight into the artists' motives.

As this is neither a devotional work nor a study of interpretation, the subject has been treated only from the legendary and picturesque point of view, and it is sincerely hoped that this fact will be duly borne in mind.

Artists and authors having found in these legends such a fruitful source of interest and inspiration, we venture to present them to the public, trusting they will receive a kindly welcome in their new dress.

CONTENTS.

CHAPTER I.

YOUTH OF THE VIRGIN MARY.

PAGE

Mary in the Bible — Legends in the first century — Crusaders bring legends west — The character of the legends — Prominence attained by Mary — Marriage of Joachim and Anna — Their sorrow — The offering refused — Joachim's penance — Anna's two visions — Joachim's vision and sacrifice — Joachim's return — The meeting at the Golden Gate — The immaculate conception of Mary — Nativity of the Virgin — Presentation of the Virgin — The priests' dispute — Mary's life in the Temple — Description of Mary — Her suitors — Her vow — The high priest's perplexity — The instructions he receives — Judah chosen by lot — The calling of the unmarried men — The story of Joseph — The rods on the altar — The priest's dismay — The flowering rod — The dove — Marriage of the Virgin — The disappointed suitor   1

CHAPTER II.

THE ANNUNCIATION.

Mary's companions — Joseph leaves Mary at Nazareth — Work for the Temple — Mary chosen by lot — The vision of Zacharias — The maidens mock Mary — The council in Heaven — The Annunciation — The Ave Maria — The meaning of the rosary — The Immaculate Conception — The doctrine in Spain — A Mohammedan legend — The work finished — Mary's journey — The Salutation — The Magnificat — The Visitation — Miracle in the garden — The birth of St. John — Mary's return home — Joseph's doubts — The high priest's summons — The waters of jealousy — The legend of the cherry-tree 23

CHAPTER III.

THE NATIVITY.

The prophecies — The portents — The Temple of Peace — The Tiburtine Sibyl — The Church of Ara Coeli — The three suns — The balsam — The date — Christmas — Cæsar's decree — The journey to Bethlehem — The two people — The cave — Joseph in search of aid — The suspense of nature — The birth of Christ — Adoration of angels — Legend of sainfoin — Zelomi and Salome — The Vision of the Shepherds — Adoration of the Shepherds — The ox and the ass — The Feast of the Ass — The circumcision — The purification — The presentation in the Temple — Simeon and Anna — Septuagint legend — Mary's first sorrow 40

CHAPTER IV.

THE FLIGHT.

Balaam's prophecy — The Magi — The three miracles — The star — Arrival at Jerusalem — Herod and the cock — Adoration of the Magi — Departure of the Magi — Subsequent career of the Magi — The wrath of Herod — The massacre of the Innocents — The flight of Elizabeth — The murder of Zacharias — Joseph warned — The flight into Egypt — The wheat field — The pine and juniper — The roses of Jericho — The aspen — The wild beasts 64

CHAPTER V.

THE SOJOURN IN EGYPT.

The road followed — The brigands — The captives released — The good thief — The robbers' den — The palm — The fountain — The arrival in Egypt — The fallen idols — The conversion of the Egyptians — The priest's son — The Sphinx — The visit to Pharaoh — The dumb bride — The leper girl — The story of the mule — The sojourn at Matarea — The sycamore — The shadow of the cross — Miraculous cures — Bartholomew — Judas — The fortune teller — Christ's playmates — The dead fish — The Egyptian teacher 85

CHAPTER VI.

THE BOYHOOD OF CHRIST.

The return to Nazareth — Christ and St. John — The broken pitcher — The children refuse to play — The story of the kids — The young king — Simon Zelotes — The seven pools — The sparrows — Two boys slain — The wrathful parents — The miracles — The education of Jesus — Zaccheus — Levi — The fruit tree — The roof accident — The dead babe — The sojourn at Jericho — The grain — The lions — The bedstead — The throne — The sojourn at Capernaum — The dead man restored — The sojourn at Bethlehem — James cured — The mason — Christ's home life — The dyer — The twelve year old Christ at Jerusalem 107

CHAPTER VII.

THE MINISTRY OF CHRIST.

PAGE

History of Joseph the Carpenter — Joseph warned of death — Joseph's request — Mary's plea to Christ — The angels receive Joseph's soul — Joseph shrouded — The burial of Joseph — Christ's promise — Christ the carpenter — The Shadow of the Cross — The Baptism — The Temptation — The wedding at Cana — The wine measure — The goose — The woodpecker — The Virgin's terror — Story of Abgar — Description of Christ — The parting of Christ and His Mother — The Passion Play — The birth of Judas — Crimes and repentance of Judas — The treachery of Judas — The death of Judas — Judas in hell — The colour of Judas — The seamen and Judas — Leonardo da Vinci's Judas 129

CHAPTER VIII.

THE PASSION WEEK.

The Last Supper — Lucifer's crown — Revolt of Lucifer — Man's downfall planned — The legend of Israfil — Banishment of Adam and Eve — The Holy Grail — The blood of Christ — Joseph in prison — Vespasian and Getus — Veronica's handkerchief — The first crusade — The Holy Grail in France — The Round Table — The Siege Perilous — The Holy Grail in England — Christ before Pilate — The officer — The standards — Procla's dream — The witnesses — The sentence 160

CHAPTER IX.

THE CRUCIFIXION.

PAGE

The willow-tree — The birch-tree — The crown of thorns — Legend of the robin — The roses — Legend of the Cross — Seth's visit to Paradise — Seth's vision — The three seeds — Solomon and the tree — The Queen of Sheba — The pool of Bethesda — The legend of Golgotha — Constantine's cross — Constantine's conversion — Helena's conversion — Helena's dream — The finding of the Cross — The Cross in Persia — Heraclius and the Cross — The Invention of the Cross — The lance of Longinus — The three nails — The cross-bill . 179

CHAPTER X.

DEATH, BURIAL, AND RESURRECTION OF CHRIST.

The Wandering Jew in fiction — The legend of the Wandering Jew — The Wandering Jew in Europe — The Crucifixion — The seamless coat — The legend of Pilate — The penitent thief — The fallen idols — The descent from the Cross — The Pieta — The entombment — La Pâmoison — The Jews' decision — Joseph imprisoned — Guards at the sepulchre — Joseph missing — The guards' defence — The Ascension — The rumours — The search for Christ — The finding of Joseph — Joseph's account of his escape 199

CHAPTER XI.

THE DESCENT INTO HADES.

The sons of Simeon — The Jews ask for their account — The writing of their statement — The dead in Hades — The Light — The prophecies — The plans of Hades and Satan — The story of Lazarus — The defence of Hades — The King of Glory — The entrance of Christ — The submission of Hades — Satan bound — The righteous delivered — Christ appears to Mary — Christ appears to James — Christ leads the redeemed to Paradise — Enoch, Elijah, and the good thief — The two versions — Pilate sees report — Herod's letter — The doom of Herodias — The death of Herod — The death of Pilate 215

CHAPTER XII.

ASSUMPTION AND CORONATION OF THE VIRGIN.

Mary at the Ascension — The seven sorrows of the Virgin — Pentecost — The Holy Ghost — Disciples take leave of the Virgin — The Annunciation — The palm — The disciples — Mary's farewell — The Virgin's soul — The shrouding of the Virgin — The funeral of the Virgin — The High Priest — The burial of the Virgin — The Assumption — Thomas' doubts — The girdle — The Coronation — The privilege granted to Mary — The last Judgment 230

CHAPTER XIII.

MOTHER AND SON IN ART.

PAGE

Christ the model man — Mary the model woman — Christ in early Christian art — The symbols by which He was represented — Pagan and Biblical types of Christ — The Good Shepherd — The Virgin in early art — The disputes and schisms in the Church — The first portrait of the Virgin — John of Damascus — The influence of the Crusades — Saint Bernard's vision — The Church plays — The influence exerted by the Renaissance — The symbols of Mary — The legend of the rose — The names of Mary — The vesture of Mary and Christ — The Madonnas — Our Lady of the Snow — Our Lady of Loretto — Our Lady of the Pillar — Our Lady of the Chair — Series of pictures — The Incoronata — The Mater Dolorosa — The Pieta — The Mater Amabilis — Plants connected with Christ — Plants connected with Mary — Conclusion 242

LIST OF ILLUSTRATIONS.

	PAGE
MADONNA AND CHILD. *Mignard* . . . *Frontispiece.*	
PRESENTATION OF THE VIRGIN IN THE TEMPLE. *Guido Reni*	11
SAINT ANNA AND THE VIRGIN MARY. *Müller* .	13
MARRIAGE OF THE VIRGIN. *Raphael*	21
ANNUNCIATION	23
IMMACULATE CONCEPTION. *Murillo*	31
SIMEON AND THE INFANT CHRIST	59
ADORATION OF THE KINGS. *Pfannschmidt* . . .	71
FLIGHT INTO EGYPT. *Van Dyck*	89
REPOSE IN EGYPT. *Merson*	95
CHRIST DISPUTING WITH THE DOCTORS. *Hoffmann*	128
THE SHADOW OF DEATH. *Holman Hunt* . . .	136
CHRIST TAKES LEAVE OF HIS MOTHER. *Plockhorst*	148
SAINT MICHAEL	161
THE CRUCIFIXION. *Michael Angelo*	189
VISION OF SAINT HELENA	193
CHRIST BEARING THE CROSS. *Raphael*	201

	PAGE
MATER DOLOROSA. *Guido Reni*	206
DESCENT INTO HADES	221
ASSUMPTION OF THE VIRGIN. *Titian*	237
CORONATION OF THE VIRGIN	240
PREDESTINATION OF THE VIRGIN. *Müller* . . .	255
MADONNA DI SAN SISTO. *Raphael*	261
MADONNA DELLA SEDIA. *Raphael*	267

CHAPTER I.

YOUTH OF THE VIRGIN MARY.

Mary in the Bible — Legends in the first century — Crusaders bring legends west — The character of the legends — Prominence attained by Mary — Marriage of Joachim and Anna — Their sorrow — The offering refused — Joachim's penance — Anna's two visions — Joachim's vision and sacrifice — Joachim's return — The meeting at the Golden Gate — The immaculate conception of Mary — Nativity of the Virgin — Presentation of the Virgin — The priests' dispute — Mary's life in the Temple — Description of Mary — Her suitors — Her vow — The high priest's perplexity — The instructions he receives — Judah chosen by lot — The calling of the unmarried men — The story of Joseph — The rods on the altar — The priest's dismay — The flowering rod — The dove — Marriage of the Virgin — The disappointed suitor.

THE Scriptures give us but little information about the Virgin Mary, and while the spurious gospels quote the Bible very freely, they add so many details derived from tradition and a very lively imagination, that they have never been considered worthy of credence by learned Christians.

The unlettered majority, however, debarred from all access to the canonical works which existed at first only in manuscript form, and were very rare indeed, obtained all their information from priests, often not more learned than themselves, and from strolling minstrels and poets.

Legendary stories about Christ and the Virgin Mary were current in the East from the very beginning of the Apostles' ministry, and were brought into the West by missionaries and returning pilgrims.

The Crusades, drawing the East and the West into close contact, gave an immense impetus to the spread of these stories, which became the favorite theme of poets and preachers, the basis of all dramatic representations, and after influencing the literature of the day, left indelible traces upon the art of the period.

The Scriptures are not, and have never been considered, a mere biography of Our Lord, of whose life they relate only as much as is necessary to satisfy His followers that He is the Son of God, and to set forth His doctrine.

This brevity was, of course, displeasing to the early Christians. Longing to know more than the canonical works contain, they gave ready credence to all the mythical details which were gradually added to the authentic narrative.

That these additions were false and fantastic,

frequently illogical, and even at times very irreverent, did not occur to their simple minds. Like little children, they ascribed to the Deity their own passions and feelings, and hence were not shocked by tales which described Jesus as mischievous, and even on occasions as downright malevolent.

As time passed on, the Virgin Mary, blessed among women, began to take a more and more prominent position in the narratives which chained the devout attention of old and young, and finally the following tale was evolved.

In the city of Nazareth, there was a man named Joachim. He was exceedingly rich, and when only twenty years of age he married Anna, a woman of Bethlehem. Both husband and wife were of the royal race, and prided themselves upon being direct descendants of King David.

Joachim and Anna were pure and righteous, and "they served the Lord with singleness of heart." Their property was always scrupulously divided into three equal parts, of which one was set aside for the Lord's service, the second bestowed upon the poor, and the third reserved for their own maintenance and that of their household.

Years passed by in unbroken peace and prosperity, but Joachim and Anna secretly mourned, because at the end of twenty years they were still childless, a state of affairs which was considered a curse among the chosen people.

At the Feast of the Dedication, Joachim went up to the temple, as was his custom, to make an offering to the Lord. His gift was twice as large as usual, but his heart was heavy as he thought of again renewing the frequently-uttered prayer for offspring.

He was about to lay his sacrifice upon the altar with the wonted ceremonies, when the high priest, who is called Issachar, Zacharias, or Reuben, according to different versions of the story, came toward him and rejected it, saying: "It is not lawful for thee to bring thine offering, seeing thou hast not begot issue in Israel."

Not content with this reproof, administered in the temple, on a solemn occasion, and in presence of the assembled people, the irate high priest drove Joachim out of the sacred inclosure.

Sorrowful and deeply ashamed, for many of his own kin had heard the loud-spoken accusation, Joachim slowly went down the temple steps. Then we are told that he hastened to the place where the registers of the Twelve

Tribes were kept, although it is a historical fact that the Twelve Tribes had long ceased to exist as such at that time.

Here Joachim carefully studied the records, and acquired the painful conviction that the high priest had told the truth, and that he alone, among all the righteous men of Israel, remained childless. This discovery was a great blow to him. He felt ashamed and accursed, and instead of returning to his home at Nazareth, he wended his way to a distant pasture, where shepherds were minding his flocks.

Arrived in mountain solitude, Joachim built a rude booth or hut, because he intended to remain there in fasting and prayer until the Lord looked mercifully upon him, and removed the curse under which he suffered so sorely.

In the mean while his wife Anna, left alone at home, mourned both her widowhood and childlessness. But her handmaiden, Judith, finally roused her from her sorrowful meditations, and bringing her a fillet, bade her bind up her hair and adorn herself in her wedding garments. Anna refused at first to hearken to this well-meant advice, and fancied that her handmaiden was mocking her; but she finally yielded to Judith's persuasions, and donned her bridal attire.

It was about the ninth hour of the day when her toilet was completed, and she wandered out into the garden which surrounded her house. Her heart was still heavy, so she seated herself under a laurel-tree and listlessly gazed upward.

In the branches above her head was a nest, and as her eyes fell upon the young sparrows in it she burst into tears, and cried aloud, "Alas! and woe is me! . . . to what shall I be likened? I cannot be likened to the fowls of heaven, for the fowls of heaven are fruitful in thy sight, O Lord! Woe is me! to what shall I be likened? Not to the unreasoning beasts of the earth, for they are fruitful in thy sight, O Lord! Woe is me! to what shall I be likened! Not to these waters, for they are fruitful in thy sight, O Lord. Woe is me! to what shall I be likened? Not unto the earth, for the earth bringeth forth her fruit in due season, and praiseth thee, O Lord."

Thus every sight and sound seemed to add poignancy to her sorrow, and made her wail aloud. Her complaint was scarcely finished, however, when an angel of the Lord suddenly appeared before her, saying: "Anna, thy prayer is heard. Thou shalt bring forth, and thy child shall be blessed throughout the whole world."

In her joy at these welcome tidings, Anna

made a solemn vow to dedicate the promised offspring, whether man-child or maid, to the service of the Lord. Then she went into her chamber, and while she knelt there, absorbed in prayer, in joyful anticipations, and in fervent thanksgivings, another angel appeared to warn her that Joachim, her husband, was even then on his way home from the sheepcotes, where a similar promise had been made to him.

Admonished by the angel to go forth and meet her husband at the Golden Gate, Anna lost no time, but hastened thither to receive Joachim's joyful greeting.

Joachim's experiences, in the mean while, had been equally blissful; for after a long period of fasting, which varying authorities limit to forty days or to five months, he too had been roused from painful meditations by the touch and appearance of a celestial messenger.

In his first astonishment Joachim remained motionless, but when he would have fallen at the feet of the radiant stranger and adored him, the angel bade him desist. The heavenly visitor then went on to announce that he had been sent to tell Joachim that the Lord had taken compassion upon him, and that he would soon be the father of a daughter destined to serve the Lord in his temple.

In his joy and gratitude at this news, Joachim would fain have shown hospitality to the angel. But the latter refused all proffer of meat and drink, and directed Joachim to build an altar and make a burnt-offering to the Lord. Encouraged by the presence of the angel, Joachim, the shepherd, ventured to take upon him the priestly office, and after erecting a rude altar, he laid upon it a lamb without a blemish.

When all was ready, and while Joachim knelt at the foot of his improvised altar, the victim was miraculously set afire, and the celestial messenger rose up to heaven with the smoke and perfume of the sacrifice which had thus been offered upon the lonely hillside.

Rapt in prayer and full of thanksgiving, Joachim remained upon his knees until evening, when his returning shepherds, frightened by his immobility, ventured to approach and to rouse him. Joachim then told them of his angelic visitor, and of the joyful promise which he had received.

Some versions of the story state that Joachim tarried upon the mountain until the angel again appeared to him and bade him go down, while others aver that he immediately began his homeward journey, which took him no less than thirty days to accomplish. He was accompanied by his shepherds, who brought the best of his flocks for a thank-offering to the Lord, and by other attendants, who carried doves for the same purpose.

As Joachim drew near the Golden Gate, which artists depict as the gate of the city, temple, or house, as fancy prompts them, he saw his wife, and, running forward to meet her, they exchanged a joyful kiss, to which some old writers aver that the Virgin owed her being.

This meeting between Joachim and Anna has often been the theme of artists, and one old master (Giotto) represents an angel hovering over husband and wife, and drawing their heads together for the chaste salute, while their admiring domestics are standing in the background with the doves and sheep.

After spending one whole day at home with his wife, to whom he doubtless gave a minute description of his angelic visitor, Joachim again went to the temple at Jerusalem, and this time his offering was not refused. There, too, his heart was further gladdened by a favorable sign, which appeared on the sacred plate which the high priest wore on his forehead.

The promise, so solemnly made to both Joachim and Anna, was duly fulfilled, and they became the parents of a beautiful little daughter whom they called Mary, which in Hebrew is Miriam. The neighbours all crowded around them to congratulate them upon the birth of this long-desired child, and hence in pictures representing the Nativity of the Holy Virgin, we often see a group of admiring women around the new-born babe.

Anna watched over the infant Mary with great tenderness, and mindful of her vow to dedicate her to the Lord as soon as she was old enough to do without a mother's care, she " made of her bedchamber a holy place, allowing nothing that was common or unclean to enter in."

None but the purest and gentlest maidens of Israel were permitted to wait upon little Mary, who, when only six months of age, was able to walk and took seven steps. When she saw this, Anna clasped her child to her bosom with rapture, and vowed that Mary should not set foot to the ground again, until she walked to the sanctuary to keep the vow which her mother had made.

When Mary was three years old, her parents felt that it was time to give up the child, as they had promised. They therefore made a great feast, to which all their friends and neighbours were invited, and when it was over, Joachim said: " Let us invite the daughters of Israel,

PRESENTATION OF THE VIRGIN IN THE TEMPLE. (Guido Reni.)

and they shall take each a taper or a lamp, and attend on her, that the child may not turn back from the temple of the Lord."

Thus escorted by her playmates, Mary, clad in blue or in pure white, went for the first time to Jerusalem. The women's court was separated from the altar by a flight of fifteen steps, which were intended as symbols of the Psalms of Degrees, that is to say, the Psalms from the one hundred and twentieth to the one hundred and thirty-fourth inclusive.

Without waiting for Anna, who was exchanging her travel-soiled garment for one of immaculate purity, the infant Mary, without one thought of fear, eagerly went up the steps alone. At the head of the flight, stood the high priest, in full pontifical array, and he kissed and blessed the child, saying: "Mary, the Lord hath magnified thy name to all generations, and in thee shall be made known the redemption of the children of Israel."

Then took place the real Presentation of the Virgin, for the priest led her to the altar, where, we are quaintly told, "she danced with her feet, so that all the house of Israel rejoiced with her, and loved her." Her parents left her there and went home rejoicing, because she had not turned away from the house of the Lord.

Such was the beauty and attractiveness of the child thus committed to their care, that twenty-five of the priests claimed the honour of watching over her, and began to dispute together concerning it. After much discussion, they agreed that the matter should be decided by lot, and going down to the Jordan in a body, each flung an arrow into the stream.

Only one of the arrows floated, that of the high priest Zacharias, and Mary was therefore entrusted to his sole care. From the very first he felt that the charge was sacred, and one of the legends relates that he kept her behind seven locked doors so that no one could gain access to her.

Notwithstanding these extraordinary precautions, the angels, who had been present at Mary's birth, and had hovered around her ever since, constantly visited her behind the fast closed doors, and although the high priest never saw them, he was mystified by the daily appearance of fresh fruits and flowers in her room.

Another version relates, that Mary grew up with the other maidens in the temple, under the watchful eye of Anna, the prophetess, who, inspired by the Holy Ghost, foretold her glorious destiny. All the versions agree however in saying that " Mary was in the temple as if she were

ST. ANNA AND THE VIRGIN MARY.
(MÜLLER.)

a dove that lived there, and she received food from the hand of an angel." As for the usual portion of food set aside for her by the high priest, she always gave it to the poor.

Mary's time in the temple was spent very methodically. From early morning until the third hour of the day, she remained in prayer; then she worked with her young companions until the ninth hour; after which she again resorted to prayer, until an angel brought her food from heaven, and bade her retire.

In pictures representing Mary in the temple, we see her spinning and weaving, embroidering the priestly garments, and receiving from angel visitors fruits or flowers from heaven, or a loaf, and a pitcher of water, intended to represent the bread and water of life.

A much discussed point in olden times was whether Mary, who is considered as the emblem of wisdom, knew everything by intuition, or whether she was educated by the angels, by her mother, and by Anna, the prophetess. This matter has never been satisfactorily decided, so in art she is sometimes represented as standing at her mother's knee, and receiving instruction, while angels hover above her with flowers and fruit.

Mary remained in the temple from three to

twelve, fourteen, or sixteen years of age, according to different authorities. We are told that she was so beautiful that "scarcely any one could gaze upon her countenance," and the description of her appearance which, owing to its antiquity, seems the most likely to be accurate, runs as follows: "She was of middle stature; her face oval; her eyes brilliant, and of an olive tint; her eyebrows arched and black; her hair was of a pale brown; her complexion fair as wheat. She spoke little, but she spoke freely and affably; she was not troubled in her speech, but grave, courteous, tranquil. Her dress was without ornament, and in her deportment was nothing lax or feeble."

Artists have, however, never followed this description slavishly, all preferring to depict the Virgin Mary according to the dictates of their fancy; and hence the great variety of Virgin types which are to be found in every picture gallery or collection of works of art.

The Virgin Mary was so pure, simple, and holy, that she is said to have enjoyed the privilege, never granted to a woman before or since, of freely entering into the Holy of Holies, where the high priest himself only ventured once a year. Here she spent her hours of prayer, and on this account the ark of the covenant is sometimes seen in the background of paintings representing her at this stage of her career.

Many miracles are ascribed to Mary during her prolonged sojourn in the temple. For instance, all who were ill were healed by merely touching her. Notwithstanding this supernatural power, and the fact that she alone, among all the virgins who dwelt in the temple, conversed with and was fed by the angels, Mary remained both modest and quiet, and diligently laboured to finish all the work which her companions left undone.

The fame of Mary's beauty and virtue was soon noised abroad, and when she grew up there was no lack of ardent suitors for her hand. Among others, the priest Abiathar came to woo in behalf of his son, offering to the high priest many rich gifts to induce him to favour his suit.

These offers were all laid before Mary, who repeated again and again that she had no intention of marrying, but that she wished to remain in the temple and serve the Lord. Her young companions, however, followed the usual custom, and left the temple as soon as they were of marriageable age to found homes of their own.

Mary's obstinate refusal to do as they did troubled the high priest greatly. Such a case had never presented itself before, and while on the one hand the law expressly forbade keeping the maidens in the temple after a certain age, on the other it was written, "When thou vowest a vow unto God, defer not to pay it."

The high priest was in a quandary. In his perplexity he assembled the priests and Levites, and laid the matter before them, imploring them to help him with their advice. The matter was discussed at length in solemn council, but they were as far from a decision as ever, when a mysterious voice was heard in the sanctuary, bidding Zacharias enter into the Holy of Holies and pray there for guidance.

According to another version of the story, no voice was heard, but the priests themselves hit upon this expedient. Whether it came from a hidden adviser, or from the council, the suggestion was received with joy, and the high priest made haste to enter into the holy place, where he breathed forth an ardent prayer for help.

While he was praying thus, "behold, the angel of the Lord stood by, saying unto him, 'Zacharias, Zacharias, go forth and summon the widowers of the people, and let them take a rod apiece, and she shall be the wife of him to whom the Lord shall show a sign.'"

A third version of the self-same story makes

no mention of priestly council or deliberations, but states that it was during the night, and while the high priest was sleeping, that an angel appeared to him. The celestial messenger bade him assemble the widowers and bachelors in Israel, and told him that a sign would reveal the man who alone was worthy of acting as guardian to the Virgin Mary, and to protect her so she could keep her vow.

When morning dawned, the high priest related his vision to Mary, who, with her usual gentle acquiescence, expressed her readiness to do the Lord's will. Next the high priest resorted to a practice common among the Jews, and ordered that lots should be cast to discover in which tribe Mary's future protector should be found.

The choice thus fell upon the tribe of Judah. Then the criers were sent forth, with the Lord's trumpet, to summon all the marriageable men to the temple of Jerusalem, where the high priest wished to see them, and whither they were expressly told to bring their rods or wands.

The summons was obeyed with great promptitude, and one of the accounts states that Joseph, the carpenter, dropping his axe and catching up his wand, rushed in breathless haste to the temple. As soon as he crossed the threshold of his shop, or of the temple, a dove appeared by miracle upon the tip of his staff, and thus the promised sign was granted.

Other versions, however, relate that Joseph obeyed the summons very reluctantly, for he was already a very old man. He had married at forty, and lived forty-nine years with his wife, who had died, after giving him four sons, Judas, Justus, James, and Simeon, and two daughters, Assia and Lydia.

Some of Joseph's children had already been married for some time, and one tradition says that, as he had grandchildren who were older than the Virgin Mary, he deemed it absurd to lay claim to her hand.

Other writers, however, remembering how important it was that the coming Redeemer should have a protector strong enough to defend Him during His helpless infancy, and capable of supplying the family wants even in a foreign land, assert that Joseph at this time was only forty, instead of eighty years of age.

One of the books of the Apocrypha tells us, therefore, that Joseph presented himself with the other candidates, although somewhat reluctant, and that when they were all assembled, the priest took their rods, which he carried into the holy place, and laid upon the altar.

There the rods remained, until he offered up a prayer unto the Lord, or until the next morning, while their owners spent the night on their knees in the outer temple. Then the high priest, full of faith in the promise of the Lord, brought out the rods and gave them back to the suitors, eagerly watching for the promised sign.

Imagine his disappointment, therefore, when the last rod had been restored, and the promised sign was still delayed. In his perplexity the high priest re-entered the holy place, and there, after renewed supplications, the angel again appeared, repeated the promise, and quoted the prophecy of Isaiah: " And there shall come forth a rod out of the stem of Jesse, and a branch shall grow out of his roots; and the Spirit of the Lord shall rest upon him, the spirit of wisdom and understanding, the spirit of counsel and might, the spirit of knowledge and of the fear of the Lord."

The angel next bade the high priest look on the altar, where he would find a short rod, which he had overlooked in his eagerness to witness the promised sign. The high priest obeyed, and found there, as he had been told, a tiny rod. When he picked it up he saw that, like Aaron's, it had budded and blossomed during the night.

The flowering rod was quickly carried out to

the waiting people and handed to Joseph, who had kept quietly in the background, because he felt himself unworthy of the honour of caring for one of the virgins dedicated to the service of the Lord.

As the rod touched his reluctant hand, some authorities claim that a second miracle took place, for a snowy dove sprang up from the staff, alighted for a moment upon his head, and then flew up to the topmost pinnacle of the temple. After pausing there for a moment, in full view of all the assembled suitors, the bird winged its way up into the sky, where it was soon lost to sight.

In representing this scene some artists have made use of one or the other version of the legend, while others, anxious to introduce all the picturesque features, have represented Joseph holding a rod covered with leaves and flowers, and surmounted by a dove, the emblem of the Holy Ghost.

> "From Jesse's root behold a branch arise,
> Whose sacred flower with fragrance fills the skies;
> Th' ethereal Spirit o'er its leaves shall move,
> And on its top descends the mystic Dove."
> *The Messiah.* — POPE.

In spite of the double miracle, which had thus plainly designated him as the destined pro-

MARRIAGE OF THE VIRGIN. (Raphael.)

tector of the Virgin, Joseph refused to accept her hand until the high priest sternly admonished him. The priest bade him make haste and obey the commands of the Lord, lest he should incur the awful punishment which had visited Korah, Abiram, and Dathan.

Thus warned of the peril of disobedience, Joseph dared make no further objections, and he was publicly betrothed to the Virgin Mary. As this was a civil contract among the Jews, the betrothal, or marriage, as it is indifferently called in legend and art, was celebrated in the open air.

The ceremony was, however, accompanied by the usual festivities and pomp, and we are told that the Virgin wore a marriage robe of precious texture. "The ground was of the colour of nankeen, with flowers blue, white, violet, and gold." This garment, first preserved as a precious treasure in Palestine, was sent to Constantinople in the fifth century, and was given, in 877, by Charles the Bald, to the Church of Chartres, where it can still be seen.

It is also claimed that an onyx and emerald ring was used for the ceremony of betrothal. This golden circlet, to which miraculous powers are ascribed, as well as to the robe, is kept in the Cathedral of Perugia. Here it is known as the Virgin's Betrothal Ring, and is regarded with much veneration.

Among the witnesses of the marriage were all the rejected suitors, and the legend relates that Abiathar's son was so disappointed at failing to secure the hand of the Virgin, that he broke his rod in anger. Not content with this public demonstration, he furthermore withdrew to a hermitage on Mount Carmel, where he spent the remainder of his life in complete seclusion, and thus became the founder of the Carmelite Order of monks.

CHAPTER II.

THE ANNUNCIATION.

Mary's companions — Joseph leaves Mary at Nazareth — Work for the Temple — Mary chosen by lot — The vision of Zacharias — The maidens mock Mary — The council in Heaven — The Annunciation — The Ave Maria — The meaning of the rosary — The Immaculate Conception — The doctrine in Spain — A Mohammedan legend — The work finished — Mary's journey — The Salutation — The Magnificat — The Visitation — Miracle in the garden — The birth of St. John — Mary's return home — Joseph's doubts — The high priest's summons — The waters of jealousy — The legend of the cherry-tree.

JOSEPH had married Mary much against his will, and had publicly assumed the responsibility of guarding her from all harm. He had evidently heard so many tales of her virtue, and of the miracles which she wrought, that he stood somewhat in awe of her. So he begged the high priest that some of the temple virgins might go with her to keep her company.

Five or seven maidens were selected for this duty, and Mary went with Joseph to Nazareth. Here, according to different versions, she either dwelt in the house of her parents, which she had inherited after Joachim's death, or in the humble home of Joseph the Carpenter, where she acted as mother to his youngest son, James, and thus won the appellation bestowed upon her in the Bible, " Mary, the mother of James."

All the versions agree, however, in stating that Joseph merely brought her into his house, where he left her, saying : " Behold, I have received thee from the temple of the Lord, and now I leave thee in my house and go to build my buildings, and will come to thee. The Lord will protect thee."

Whether Mary remained thus alone with her companions a few months or two years is a matter of dispute also ; but the next salient point in the narrative leads us back to the temple at Jerusalem. The priests, again assembled in council, had decided to have a new curtain made for the temple of the Lord. But the work could be done by certain persons only, and the high priest said : " Call me undefiled virgins of the house of David."

His servants went forth to do his bidding, and after diligent search they found Mary and seven other maidens. They were brought into the temple, told what work was expected of them, and shown the materials. Next the priest said to Mary: "Cast me lots who shall spin the gold, and green, and fine linen, and silk, and blue, and scarlet, and true purple."

Mary obeyed, and when the true purple and scarlet fell to her share, she reverently carried it home and began her work, which must have extended over a period of several months.

The apocryphal writings only allude to the apparition of the angel to Zacharias in the temple, and to the Scriptural promise: "Fear not, Zacharias, for thy prayer is heard, and thy wife Elizabeth shall bear thee a son, and thou shalt call his name John. And thou shalt have joy and gladness, and many shall rejoice at his birth. For he shall be great in the sight of the Lord, and shall drink neither wine nor strong drink; and he shall be filled with the Holy Ghost, even from his mother's womb. And many of the children of Israel shall he turn to the Lord their God. And he shall go before him in the spirit and power of Elias, to turn the hearts of the fathers to the children, and the disobedient to the wisdom of the just; to make ready a people prepared for the Lord."

This whole scene, so graphically described by Saint Luke, and which has been the subject of many a painting, is dismissed in the spurious gospels with the few words: "And at that time

Zacharias became speechless, and Samuel was in his stead, until Zacharias spake."

Mary, as we have seen, had taken her work home, where her companions, jealous that the choicest materials had fallen to her share, began to taunt her, and mockingly called her "Queen of the Virgins." This raillery gradually increased, and they even began to bow down to her and to do her pretended obeisance.

As usual, Mary remained gentle and humble, so her companions continued their taunts until an angel appeared to them and bade them refrain. He further told them that the title, "Queen of the Virgins," which they had given Mary in derision, was prophetic of her future exalted position.

Silenced and terrified by this unwonted reproof, the maidens humbly begged Mary's pardon, and never again ventured to treat her with anything but the utmost deference. Mary's life, in the mean while, was quite unchanged. Her time was divided between prayer, meditation, and work, and the angels visited her daily and brought her food.

One day, after spinning diligently for the new temple veil, Mary took up her pitcher and went to the fountain to draw water to wash her hands. It was while she was thus out of doors that she heard a voice saying, "Hail, thou favoured one, the Lord is with thee, blessed art thou among women."

Astonished at hearing such a greeting in a place where she deemed herself alone, Mary looked around her to discover whence the voice came. She saw no one, however, and, taking up her pitcher, went into the house, where she resumed her work, if we are to believe one version of the tale which has come down to us.

Another version, however, says that she began reading the prophecy in Isaiah, " Behold, a virgin shall conceive, and bear a son, and shall call his name Immanuel," and that she unconsciously exclaimed aloud how happy she would be to serve as handmaiden to a woman so blessed.

The words had scarcely left her lips when the Salutation which she heard before in the garden was repeated, and looking up, she beheld a radiant angel, who cried, " Blessed art *thou* among women."

The legends, which have a quaint way of filling all gaps, gravely inform us that the time having come when the long promised Redeemer should appear in the flesh, God had assembled all his angels and made his purpose known to them. Then, wishing to apprise Mary of the honour awaiting her, he bade Gabriel go down and announce to her that she was to be the mother of the Messiah.

God chose Gabriel for this joyful embassy, to indemnify him for having been obliged in years long gone by to drive our first parents out of the Garden of Eden. The angel who had announced Paradise lost was to have the privilege of foretelling Paradise regained! Gabriel, radiant with joy, flashed down from the heavenly abode to bear this welcome message.

He was accompanied by the heavenly host; but while a few angels followed him all the way down to earth, they waited outside, while he alone went in to Mary. As emblem of his office, Gabriel, "a young man whose beauty could not be told," bore a lily without stamens, and on account of this circumstance, painters have always represented him with the blossom which is a symbol of purity, and is hence known as "Fleur de Marie."

Mary was so accustomed to heavenly visitants that she felt no fear of them at all. The angel's words alone caused the terror recorded in the Bible. The legends state that she questioned the angel, who now went on to explain to her, "The power of the Lord will overshadow thee; wherefore also that holy thing which is born of thee shall be called the son of the Most High;

THE ANNUNCIATION.

and thou shalt call his name Jesus; for he shall save the people from their sins."

Simply, humbly, and with touching faith, Mary accepted the message, whose full import she could hardly understand, and said: " Behold the servant of the Lord is before him; be it unto me according to thy word."

In many old pictures the artists have tried to emphasize the meaning of this annunciation, by representing the Heavenly Father hovering above, and, flying downward from between his outstretched arms, a diminutive figure of the Saviour bearing His cross. Others, and they are most numerous, depict a snowy dove, flashing down upon a beam of light, which falls directly upon Mary in her humble attitude of handmaiden of the Lord.

In the Middle Ages, when the worship of the Virgin had gained its strongest hold upon the people, and when she was literally placed above her Son, every detail of her life was discussed with great heat by the monks of various orders. Then, too, the decision was reached that the Annunciation took place at sunset.

"Ave Maria! blessed be the hour!
The time, the clime, the spot, where I so oft
Have felt that moment in its fullest power
Sink o'er the earth so beautiful and soft;

> While swung the deep bell in the distant tower,
> Or the faint dying day-hymn stole aloft,
> And not a breath crept through the rosy air,
> And yet the forest leaves seem'd stirr'd with prayer."
>
> BYRON.

This hour henceforth became hallowed, and was marked by the pealing of a bell, which, in memory of the angel, is known as the Angelus. It was in the 15th century that a Papal edict first enjoined the recitation, at that hour, of the Ave Maria, a prayer sacred to the Virgin Mary, and which is worded as follows : " Hail Mary, full of grace, the Lord is with thee ; blessed art thou among women, and blessed is the fruit of thy womb Jesus. Holy Mary, mother of God, pray for us sinners now, and in the hour of our death, Amen."

This prayer, which is generally used by the Roman Catholics, holds a more important place in the rosary than the Lord's prayer. For, in the larger rosary there are a series of one hundred and fifty repetitions of the " Ave Maria," with a " Pater-Noster " interpolated after each decade, while in the lesser rosary there are fifty Aves and five Pater-Nosters. The small beads in rosaries serve to keep account of the number of prayers addressed to the Blessed Virgin, while the larger ones

IMMACULATE CONCEPTION. (Murillo.)

serve to mark every recurrence of the Lord's prayer.

The Annunciation is further commemorated in the Roman Catholic Church by a very important festival, which the Church Calendar appoints to be held on the twenty-fifth of March.

To mediæval discussions, and to a doctrine of the Roman Catholic Church we further owe a style of picture, which in art is generally known as the Immaculate Conception. In these pictures, the Virgin, a young girl from twelve to sixteen years of age, is represented as caught up in the clouds, with the moon crescent under her feet and often surrounded by angels. On account of the vision of St. John, recorded in Revelations, where he beheld "a woman clothed with the sun, and the moon under her feet, and upon her head a crown of twelve stars," the Virgin is also frequently represented with the sun as a background, flooding her blue or white robe with refulgent light, and crowned with twelve stars which are symbolical of the twelve tribes of Israel.

> "Woman! above all women glorified,
>   Our tainted nature's solitary boast;
>   Purer than eastern skies at daybreak strewn
>   With fancied roses, than the unblemished moon
>   Before her wane begins on heaven's blue coast;
>   Thy Image falls to earth." WORDSWORTH.

As the Spaniards were the most zealous advocates of the doctrine of the Immaculate Conception, and claimed that the Virgin was born free from every taint of original sin, they nearly went mad with joy when the Pope, in 1617, confirmed by a solemn decree the doctrine which had long been the subject of so much dispute. "On the publication of this bull, Seville flew into a frenzy of religious joy," and the Spaniards celebrated the triumph of their long cherished belief by every imaginable festivity. And it is because this is a favourite doctrine in Spain that most of the paintings entitled the Immaculate Conception belong to the Spanish school.

A peculiar Mohammedan legend relates that Mary fled out into the desert immediately after the Annunciation, and, resting under a solitary palm-tree, gave birth to her child. A fountain sprang by miracle from the sandy soil, wherein she bathed the new-born babe, and it was said that only a few hours elapsed between the Annunciation and the Nativity.

Such is not, however, the account given by apocryphal gospels, where we read that Mary resumed her work as soon as the angel Gabriel left her. When it was all finished she carried it to the high priest, who blessed her, saying: "Mary, the Lord God hath magnified thy name, and thou shalt be blessed in all the generations of the earth."

This blessing filled her heart with joy, and with its sound still ringing in her ears, Mary arose and " went into the hill country with haste, into a city of Judah, and entered into the house of Zacharias, and saluted Elizabeth." Mary had doubtless heard of the miracle which had befallen her kinswoman, and as her own mother was dead, it was quite natural that she should thus go and see her nearest female relative.

Although Elizabeth was so much older, and such a greeting was unheard of from an aged to a young woman, she ran to meet Mary, saying, " Whence is this to me, that the mother of my Lord should come to me ?" This unexpected confirmation of the angel's promise and of the priest's blessing, united to her own conviction, filled Mary's heart with such joy that she gave vent to her thanksgiving in the hymn which is known as the Magnificat, and which St. Luke has preserved for us in his Gospel : " My soul doth magnify the Lord, and my spirit hath rejoiced in God my Saviour. For he hath regarded the low estate of his handmaiden ; for behold, from henceforth all generations shall call me blessed. For he that is mighty hath done to me great things, and Holy is his name. And his mercy is on them that fear him from generation to generation. He hath showed strength with his arm, he hath scattered the proud in the imagination of their hearts. He hath put down the mighty from their seats, and exalted them of low degree. He hath filled the hungry with good things, and the rich he hath sent empty away. He hath holpen his servant Israel in remembrance of his mercy, as he spake to our fathers, to Abraham and his seed for ever."

This "Song of the Blessed Virgin Mary has been used as the Vesper Canticle of the Church from time immemorial," and has been beautifully set to music by Palestrina, Bach, Mendelssohn, and other composers of note.

While it is generally supposed that Mary, young as she was, undertook the journey into the hill country alone, or escorted by a boy servant only, some artists assume that Joseph went with her, and represent him holding the ass upon which Mary evidently rode, and gazing in wonder at her meeting with Elizabeth. Sometimes the women embrace in the house, at other times on the door step, or even in the open air, where Scriptural subjects in the background frequently serve to connect the Old Testament with the New, or foreshadow some important event in the life of Christ or of John the Baptist.

Mary's sojourn in Elizabeth's house, which is generally known as the Visitation, is supposed to have extended over a period of several months. Mary dwelt there in great retirement, " for day by day her condition became more manifest," and she only wandered out into the garden from time to time to hold communion with nature.

One of the legends relates that while she was wandering thus among the flowers, she one day accidentally touched a blossom which until then had been inodorous. This passing contact was enough. The flower breathed forth the most exquisite perfume, and we are told it has been fragrant ever since, although the narrators of this miracle have omitted giving us the name of the plant on which it grew.

The feast of the Visitation, also observed by the Roman Catholic Church, is fixed for the second of July, which may have been the epoch when Mary's visit drew to a close. Although it is not expressly stated that Mary was present at the birth of John the Baptist, her visit extended so nearly to the time when Elizabeth's hopes were to be crowned, that some artists have ventured to represent her either holding the new-born infant, or giving the tablet to Zacharias, that he might confirm his wife's words and declare that the child should be named John.

It was just before or immediately after John's birth that Mary returned to Nazareth, where she dwelt in great seclusion until six months had gone by since the Annunciation. Then only, according to some legends, Joseph came home from the maritime countries, where he had been building tabernacles.

A family man, and the father of grandchildren, Joseph immediately perceived the state of affairs, and began to reproach Mary bitterly. She denied all his accusations, and her attendants, when questioned, testified that she had led a life of exemplary piety and retirement, receiving none but angel visits.

Joseph, silenced but unconvinced, now quietly prepared to divorce Mary. But the Scriptures tell us, "while he thought on these things, behold, the angel of the Lord appeared unto him in a dream, saying, 'Joseph, thou son of David, fear not to take unto thee Mary thy wife; for that which is conceived in her is of the Holy Ghost. And she shall bring forth a son, and thou shalt call his name JESUS, for he shall save his people from their sins.'"

Some of the legends follow this version closely, and only add that upon awakening Joseph went in search of Mary, and humbly begged her pardon for his insulting suspicions and injurious words.

> "'Bot I wot well my leman fre,
> I have trespast to god and the;
> Forgyf me, I the pray.'"
>
> *Widkirk Play.*

The Arabic legends, however, give a different account of the affair, and claim that the unborn infant raised his voice to proclaim his mother's purity and innocence, and to chide Joseph for his unbelief. Then, convinced by miracle, Joseph made no further remonstrances, but sought and obtained Mary's full and free forgiveness.

Although Joseph had been satisfied, the tongues of his neighbours daily wagged faster, and it was soon rumoured far and wide that Joseph's betrothed, as she is generally called, had broken her vow of chastity, and that he had failed to keep his promise to the high priest and guard the Virgin of the Lord.

These rumours finally came to the ears of the high priest, who, knowing Joseph was a just man, refused at first to credit them. But they soon became so persistent that the high priest sent his servant, Annas, the scribe, to Nazareth, to discover whether there was any foundation for the reports which were so rife.

The scribe returned, confirming the news, and the high priest in anger sent for Joseph and Mary, whom he questioned and reproved separately. Baffled by their answers, yet unable to believe their repeated assertions that they had in no wise violated their vows, the high priest condemned them both to drink the " waters of jealousy."

This ordeal was endured in public, and when they had safely undergone it, and walked seven times around the altar, the high priest was forced to acquit them both. Some accounts declare that after drinking the waters of jealousy, Mary, in the presence of the assembled people, uttered another grand hymn, a companion to the " Magnificat," which, however, has not been preserved for our perusal.

Thus freed from suspicion, Mary and Joseph returned home to Nazareth " glorifying the God of Israel." There, if we are to believe the legends, several extraordinary things happened, and one of these miracles is embodied in a quaint mediæval carol published in an old English chap-book. This song, of which we can quote only a few lines, begins thus: —

> " When Joseph was an old man, an old man was he,
>   And he married Mary, the Queen of Galilee;
>   When Joseph he had his cousin Mary got,
>   Mary proved with child."
>
> *Cherry-Tree Carol.*

The story then goes on rehearsing Joseph's suspicions, which he, however, wisely keeps to himself. While he and Mary were walking in their garden one day she expressed a wish for some fine red cherries hanging above her head, but Joseph roughly said the father of her child might gather them for her. Then the unborn infant spoke to his mother, saying:—

> "Go to the tree, Mary, and it shall bow down,
> And the highest branch shall bow to Mary's knee,
> And she shall gather cherries by one, two, and three."
> *Cherry-Tree Carol.*

Mary then spoke to the tree, which, as Jesus had said, bent down before her, and remained in that position until she had gathered all the cherries she wished, and made Joseph thoroughly ashamed of his churlish behaviour. It is popularly supposed that it is on account of this legend that artists sometimes represent the Virgin as amusing the Christ Child by dangling bright red cherries just within reach of his baby hands.

CHAPTER III.

THE NATIVITY.

The prophecies — The portents — The Temple of Peace — The Tiburtine Sibyl — The Church of Ara Coeli — The three suns — The balsam — The date — Christmas — Cæsar's decree — The journey to Bethlehem — The two people — The cave — Joseph in search of aid — The suspense of nature — The birth of Christ — Adoration of angels — Legend of sainfoin — Zelomi and Salome — The Vision of the Shepherds — Adoration of the Shepherds — The ox and the ass — The Feast of the Ass — The circumcision — The purification — The presentation in the Temple — Simeon and Anna — Septuagint legend — Mary's first sorrow.

THE time was now rapidly approaching when the angel's promise should be fulfilled, and the expected Redeemer be born. His coming had, as we know, long been expected by the chosen race, whose sacred books recorded many prophecies concerning him, from the words spoken by God himself in the Garden of Eden, to the last utterance of Malachi about three hundred years before.

Since then, many unauthentic prophecies had been added, such as those contained in the apocalyptic literature. Many writers further claim that Christ's coming had been also foretold to the Gentiles, by means of the prophetesses called Sibyls, who number from four to twelve, according to varying authorities, and who have been deemed worthy of a place in the magnificent decorations of the Sistine Chapel in Rome.

Many miraculous portents are further said to have occurred in all parts of the known world at this particular time. The principal one seems to have been the cessation of the constant warfare which had desolated so many countries, and the beginning of a general truce, the fit herald of the " Prince of Peace."

> " It was the calm and silent night!
>   Seven hundred and fifty-three,
> Had Rome been growing up to might,
>   And now was Queen of land and sea.
> No sound was heard of clashing wars,
>   Peace brooded o'er the hush'd domain,
> Apollo, Pallas, Jove, and Mars
>   Held undisturb'd their ancient reign.
>   In the solemn midnight
>   Centuries ago."
>   ALFRED DOMMETT.— *A Christmas Hymn.*

All the noted oracles, through whom the gods had been wont to make their wishes known, although still questioned by eager worshippers, were silent, and the heathens cried that their deities had become dumb. Then too, the nymphs and the genii of nature were heard softly bewailing themselves, for they knew that their reign was at an end.

> "The oracles are dumb,
>   No voice or hideous hum
> Runs through the arch'd roof in words deceiving.
>   Apollo from his shrine,
>   Can no more divine,
> With hollow shriek the sleep of Delphos leaving.
>   No nightly trance, or breathed spell
> Inspires the pale-eyed priest from the prophetic cell.
>
> " The lonely mountain o'er,
>   And the resounding shore,
> A voice of weeping heard and loud lament,
>   From haunted spring and dale,
>   Edged with the poplar pale,
> The parting genius is with sighing sent;
>   With flower-inwoven tresses torn
> The nymphs in twilight shade of tangled thickets mourn."
>
> MILTON. — *Hymn to the Nativity.*

Rome had at that epoch reached the zenith of its power, so most of the legends naturally refer in some way to its history. Thus we are told that at the beginning of the universal truce, twelve years before our era, the happy Romans erected a temple which they dedicated to Peace.

Desirous of ascertaining how long the building would endure, they sent to the oracle of Apollo, from whom they received the answer, " Until a virgin bring forth and remain a virgin." This oracular speech being interpreted to mean that the temple would stand forever, the Romans proudly put up the inscription " The Eternal Temple of Peace."

But, on the very night when Christ the Lord was born in Bethlehem of Judea, the Temple of Peace fell with an awful crash. At the same time a fountain of oil gushed forth from the arid soil, and flowed down into the Tiber, " in token that the Fountain of Piety and Mercy was born," and that its grace would extend to all people.

The Roman senate now offered to pay divine honours to Cæsar Augustus, because he was the first to rule over a whole world at peace. In doubt whether to accept this worship the Emperor sent for the Tiburtine Sibyl, and bade her tell him whether any one greater than he should ever be born.

The Sibyl refused to give an immediate answer, but a few days later she sought the Emperor's presence, and bidding him look upward, showed him a golden circle around the sun. Within this circumference appeared a beautiful maiden, holding a child in her lap. The Sibyl then told the emperor that the babe was greater than he, and was the first-born Son of God.

She had scarcely finished speaking, when a heavenly voice was heard to proclaim aloud, "Here is the altar of Heaven." The vision soon faded away; but the emperor, satisfied with what he had seen, not only refused the divine honours which the senate would fain have awarded him, but gave orders that an altar should be built on the eminence on which the Mother and Child had appeared. This shrine was dedicated to the "First-Born Son of God."

Some years later a Christian church was erected upon the same spot, and dedicated to the Virgin Mary. In remembrance of the vision, the church, which still stands upon the Capitoline Hill, bears the name of "Santa Maria Ara Cœli." It is reached by an imposing flight of one hundred and twenty-four steps, and among its most prized relics is a "Bambino," or Infant Saviour, carved from wood from the Mount of Olives, and painted by St. Luke.

This Bambino is exhibited in a manger on Christmas Day, and as the Romans claim that it is gifted with miraculous powers it is often carried to sick beds, and thus made a source of revenue to the church. A very ancient bas-relief represents the Tiburtine Sibyl explaining the heavenly vision to the emperor, a subject which has also been treated by several other artists of the Italian schools.

In the far East three suns appeared at once on this auspicious day, and while the people gazed upon them in awe and wonder they were seen to merge into one. Hence this phenomenon has been explained as a symbol of the Trinity.

Then, too, the vines of Engedi flowered spontaneously, and " produced balsam, in token that he was born who should preserve all things by the virtue of the stream of his blood."

Although by our present method of computing time we profess to count the years from the birth of Christ, it is not positively known when He was born. Learned investigations have pretty clearly demonstrated, however, that our era — which was introduced in Italy in the sixth century — begins in about the fourth year of our Redeemer's life.

The early Christians did not at first celebrate the Nativity, although birthday festivities were common at that time among the heathen. The anniversary of Our Lord's coming, therefore, passed almost unnoticed until about the fourth century, when it first began to be observed.

Such was the popularity of this innovation, however, that fifty years later it was adopted by all the Christians. But it became a general custom only in the thirteenth century, and was so popular among the unbelievers because it replaced the ancient Roman Saturnalia and the Northern Yule festival, which had been celebrated at the same season, and combined their feasts and customs with its deeper significance.

The twenty-fifth of December was agreed upon as a particularly auspicious day for this celebration for several other reasons. For instance, St. Augustine said John the Baptist was born on June 25th, at the summer solstice. As the great Precursor had said of Christ, " He must increase, but I must decrease," it seemed particularly appropriate that John's birthday should fall on the day when the sun begins to decrease and that of his Master on the winter solstice, or day when the sun again begins to increase. Thus the birth of the sun, and of the Sun of Righteousness were, not without a deep sense of poetical fitness, made synchronous, and served to illustrate the prophecy of Malachi : " Unto you that fear my name shall the Sun of Righteousness arise with healing in His wings."

The natural sequence of this mode of reasoning was that the Annunciation was fixed on the 25th day of March, a date which was also considered the anniversary of the Creation, because then the days and nights are of equal length, and it therefore seemed as if they best illustrated the text of Genesis, " And the evening and the morning were the first day."

Spring was chosen in preference to fall for this anniversary, because it was written that on the third day "the earth brought forth grass," a statement which is true only at the vernal period, when every year the miracle of creation is renewed to remind mankind of the origin of all things.

In the Gospels we find the statement, " And it came to pass in those days, that there went out a decree from Cæsar Augustus that all the world should be taxed." It was in obedience to this imperial order that Joseph was obliged to go to Bethlehem, where the records for the tribe of Judah were kept, so as to register himself and all his family.

The legends tell us that Joseph was in a great quandary, because he did not know how to enrol Mary; and that he started out with her leaving the matter undecided, and saying, "The day of the Lord will itself bring it about as the Lord willeth it." He was accompanied, according to some versions, by his children by his first marriage; but other accounts state that he and Mary travelled alone.

The Virgin rode upon an ass, which Joseph led, and from time to time he turned around to see how she was bearing the journey. Once he saw her tearful and distressed, and was greatly troubled lest she were suffering; but when he again looked around he was surprised to see her radiant with joy and smiling brightly.

These sudden alterations of mood in a person so calm and pensive aroused his curiosity, and he questioned her, saying, "Mary, what aileth thee, because I see thy face at one time laughing and at another time sad?" Mary said to Joseph, "I see two peoples with my eyes, one weeping and lamenting, and one rejoicing and exulting."

This answer was so far from clear that Joseph harshly reproved her for talking nonsense. But even while he was speaking there appeared before him a beautiful youth clothed in white, who said to him, "Why didst thou call superfluous the words concerning the two peoples of whom Mary hath spoken? For she saw the people of the Jews weeping, who have departed from their

God, and the people of the Gentiles rejoicing, who have now approached and are made nigh to the Lord, as he promised our fathers Abraham, Isaac, and Jacob; for the time is come that in the seed of Abraham a blessing shall be bestowed on all nations."

The Scriptural narrative of the birth of Our Lord is too familiar to need any mention here. But the legends, which, while quoting occasionally from the canonical books, vary widely, have furnished the material for so many noted works of art, that notwithstanding their evident falsity and manifold contradictions, they have attained great importance.

We are told that travelling thus slowly, the night overtook Joseph and Mary when they were still three miles from Bethlehem, and that an angel came with a lantern to guide them along their way. As Mary was too weary to proceed any further, the angel led the travellers to a cave by the wayside, where, in bygone ages, Jesse, the father of David, had sheltered his sheep.

Another version says that they came at night into Bethlehem, where they vainly knocked at every door asking for a night's shelter. The khan was full; but the porter, hearing that Joseph and Mary belonged to the house of David, and full of reverence for the descendants of that glorious king, led them into a stable hollowed out of the rocks, which was near the inn. Some writers claim that the porter was not so much impressed by the travellers' august lineage, as by the touching beauty of Mary, who implored him to find a place where she might rest.

The most ancient legends, however, generally agree with the first version, and say that Joseph, after helping Mary to dismount, bade his sons lead her into the cave, and watch over her. Then he took a lantern, and went off in haste, in search of some charitable woman who would come to their assistance at this critical time.

When he had gone a short distance, Joseph turned around, and cast an anxious glance at the cave where Mary was to find shelter. Suddenly he saw a bright light flash down from heaven, and as she entered the cave, the light seemed to pass in with her, filling its space with the radiance of noon, and shining there steadily. This miraculous light is said to have beamed there night and day as long as Mary remained in the cave, and to have surrounded her with such dazzling splendour that no human eye could gaze upon her.

Amazed by this portent, Joseph looked around him. All nature seemed to stand still in expectancy of some great event, and Joseph, relating his experiences of the time at a subsequent period, is reported to have said: "And I Joseph walked, and walked not; and I looked up into the air, and saw the air violently agitated; and I looked up at the pole of heaven, and saw it stationary, and the fowls of heaven still; and I looked at the earth, and saw a vessel lying, and workmen reclining by it, and their hands in the vessel, and those who handled it did not handle it, and those who took did not lift, and those who presented it to their mouth did not present it, but the faces of all were looking up; and I saw sheep scattered, and the sheep stood, and the shepherd lifted up his hand to strike them and his hand remained up; and I looked at the stream of the river, and I saw that the mouths of the kids were down, and not drinking and everything which was being impelled forward was intercepted in its course."

This state of general suspense and hushed expectancy, which seems so fit at this auspicious time, has been set forth in inimitable beauty and delicacy of expression by Milton, in his Hymn in honour of the Nativity, where we read: —

"But peaceful was the night
Wherein the Prince of Light
His reign of peace upon the earth began;
The winds with wonder whist,

> Smoothly the waters kissed,
> Whispering new joys to the mild ocean,
> Who now hath quite forgot to rave,
> While birds of calm sit brooding on the charmèd wave."

A few moments later, Joseph met a woman, to whom he gave a hasty explanation, and she immediately turned to accompany him back to the cave. But her services were no longer needed, for during Joseph's short absence, Mary had given birth to her Son, whom the angels immediately surrounded and were the first to worship.

The legends say that the angels were allowed this privilege, because they had been chosen to bear witness of His coming, and that the new-born child stood among them and blessed them while they adored Him, singing, "Glory to God on high, and on earth peace to men of good will." Mary, whom some traditions represent as having escaped all suffering at this time, because she alone among all women was quite free from sin, now wrapped her new-born babe in swaddling clothes, and laid Him in a manger. As His head touched the hay which formed His bed, the vegetable world also bore witness to His divinity, for we are told that the dry rose-coloured sainfoin was restored to life and beauty, and began to expand its pretty flowers, which lovingly twined into a wreath around our infant Saviour's head.

When Joseph and the nurse Zelomi crossed the threshold of the cave they stood still in wonder at the bright light, the divine babe, and the radiant mother who bent in adoration over Him. The nurse, who had heard of Mary, of her long sojourn in the temple, and of the rumours which had lately been afloat in Nazareth and Jerusalem concerning her, now exclaimed in wonder, "Can this thing be?" and Mary proudly answered, " As none among children is equal to my son, so his mother hath no equal among women."

Zelomi was so overcome by the sight of the Virgin Mother and the Holy Child, that she stepped out of the cave to recover her senses in the open air. There she met Salome, one of her cronies, to whom she imparted the whole story, and who, unconvinced by her companion's testimony, vowed that ocular demonstration alone would convince her that a virgin had given birth to a child.

The two women now entered into the cave together. Salome's doubts were dispelled, and a miracle further served to convince her of the holiness of mother and child, for it is said that as she touched Mary her hand and arm fell to her side paralysed. She cried out in fear, but Mary, or an angel of the Lord, kindly bade her stretch out her hand and touch the child believing, and she should be healed. Salome obeyed, and as her hand and arm were made whole once more she returned grateful thanks and worshipped Him. Then a voice was heard saying, "Tell not the strange things thou hast seen until the child shall enter Jerusalem," an injunction which she obeyed.

St. Luke tells us that there were "shepherds abiding in the field, keeping watch over their flock by night. And lo! the angel of the Lord came upon them, and the glory of the Lord shone round about them, and they were sore afraid. And the angel said unto them, 'Fear not; for, behold, I bring you good tidings of great joy, which shall be to all the people. For unto you is born this day, in the city of David, a Saviour which is Christ the Lord. And this shall be a sign unto you: ye shall find the babe wrapped in swaddling clothes, lying in a manger.' And suddenly there was with the angel a multitude of the heavenly host praising God, and saying, 'Glory to God in the highest, and on earth peace, good will toward men.'"

> "The sacred chorus first was sung
> Upon the first of Christmas days;
> The Shepherds heard it overhead,—
> The joyful angels rais'd it then:
> Glory to heaven on high, it said,
> And peace on earth to gentle men!"
>
> THACKERAY.

The legends, doubtless, feeling that nothing could be added to this description, which is so brief but minute, have merely given us the names of two of the shepherds, Simon and Jude, adding that they afterwards became disciples of the Lord, whose advent had thus been made known to them by the archangel Raphael. In the miracle plays, however, some rough joking is introduced here, and the shepherds play tricks upon one another.

Full of simple and unquestioning faith, the shepherds arose after this vision and went in haste to the cave, where they "found Mary and Joseph, and the babe lying in the manger."

> "The shepherds went their hasty way,
> And found the lowly stable shed
> Where the Virgin-Mother lay;
> And now they checked their eager tread,
> For to the Babe that at her bosom clung,
> A mother's song the Virgin-Mother sung.
>
> "They told her how a glorious light
> Streamed from a heavenly throng,
> Around them shone, suspending night!

> While sweeter than a mother's song,
> Blest angels heralded the Saviour's birth,
> Glory to God on high! and Peace on Earth."
>
> COLERIDGE.

In works of art representing the Nativity, the adoration of the angels, and that of the shepherds, an ox and an ass are frequently seen in the background. The introduction of these animals is not merely intended to emphasize the fact that Our Lord was born in a stable, but also to set forth the popular belief that the dumb beasts worshipped Him also.

> " We sate among the stalls at Bethlehem.
> The dumb kine, from their fodder turning them,
> Softened their horned faces
> To almost human gazes
> Toward the newly born."
>
> ELIZABETH BARRETT BROWNING.

Old writers claim that the presence of animals had been foretold in the ancient Jewish prophecies, and quote, in support of this belief, Isaiah's words: " The ox knoweth his owner, and the ass his master's crib," and a passage in Habakkuk which is rendered in the Vulgate thus: " He shall lie down between the ox and the ass." The legends therefore add that all nature bore witness to Him, and that the animals kneeling down confessed Him.

> "Ox and ass him know,
>   Kneeling on their knee;
>   Wondrous joy had I
>   This little Babe to see."
>   WM. MORRIS, *from old Christmas Carol.*

This superstition is still current among the Breton peasants, who claim that domestic animals are gifted with the power of speech at midnight on Christmas Eve. In England it was the custom in Herefordshire and elsewhere to drink the health of the cattle on Twelfth Night, calling each animal by name.

> "Here's to the champion, to the white horn;
> Here's, God send the master a good crop of corn,
> Of wheat, rye, and barley, and all sorts of grain.
> If we live to this time twelvemonth, we'll drink his health again."
>   *Wassail Pledge.*

A large cake, baked with a hole in the middle, was then hung upon the horn of the finest ox, which was tickled and goaded until it tossed its head and flung the cake off. If the cake fell behind the ox it became the property of the mistress; but if it struck the earth in front of the animal, the farm hands considered it their lawful prize.

Another mediæval belief was that the ass, an emblem of the Gentiles, brayed aloud for joy at the birth of Our Lord, while the ox, the type of the unbelieving Jews, remained stolid and unmoved. This superstition gave rise to a curious festival in honour of the ass, which had not only testified to Christ's divinity, but bore Him into Egypt, and later on, when He made His triumphant entry, into Jerusalem. On this festive occasion an ass was decked with flowers, and at mass the responses were made by imitating the animal's braying. This curious festival was, strange to relate, very popular, and was only abolished in the 16th century.

We are told that three days after the birth of Christ, Mary left the cave to take up her abode in the stable, or rude booth, constructed at its entrance. Here the Holy Family tarried three days, and on the sixth day they went either into Bethlehem, or to Jerusalem. On the seventh day the Christ Child was circumcised, according to the Jewish rite, and received the name of Jesus, a name which Origen tells us has never been borne by any sinner. Bishop Taylor says that the Saviour then received "that name before which every knee was to bow, which was to be set above the powers of magic, the mighty rites of sorcerers, the secrets of Memphis, the drugs of Thessaly, the silent and mysterious murmurs of the wise Chaldees, and the spells of

SIMEON AND THE INFANT CHRIST. (Fra Bartolommeo.)

Zoroaster; that name which we should engrave on our hearts, and pronounce with our most harmonious accents, and rest our faith on, and place our hopes in, and love with the overflowing of charity, joy, and adoration."

Thirty-three days after the Circumcision, and forty days after the Birth of Christ, took place the Purification of the Virgin Mary, and the Presentation of Christ in the temple. The Mosaic law exacted that a first-born son should be redeemed by the offering of five shekels if the parents were rich, or by a pair of young pigeons if they were poor.

As Mary and Joseph belonged to the poorer class she brought two doves to the temple, and having gone through the prescribed ceremonies for the purification of women after childbirth, Mary brought the infant Jesus into the temple. There the Child was welcomed by the aged prophetess Anna, who foretold that He had come to redeem the people. But, as she refrained from taking Him in her arms, she is considered a type of the synagogue, which prophesied about the Messiah, but did not embrace Him when He appeared.

Simeon, on the contrary, is considered the type of the Gentiles, who not only testified to the Lord's coming, but were eager to follow His teachings. While this scene is described in a few beautiful verses in the Scriptures, tradition adds several curious details to the account.

We are told that, about two hundred and eighty years before, Ptolemy was anxious to have the Hebrew Scriptures translated into Greek, so that he might place them in his famous library at Alexandria. He therefore sent a message to Eleazar, the high priest of the Jews, asking him to send scribes and learned rabbis to his court to do that work.

Eleazar selected six of the most learned men from each of the twelve tribes of Israel, and sent them to Egypt. These seventy-two men, among whom was Simeon, an erudite priest, were warmly welcomed by Ptolemy, and were put in a quiet retreat on the island of Pharos, where they laboured diligently.

Some versions say that each of these rabbis was required to translate all the Jewish canon, a piece of work which was accomplished in seventy-two weeks, or even in seventy-two days, according to different authorities. This translation, which from the number of scribes and the time employed in making it is known as the Septuagint version, was so accurate, that all the copies were alike word for word, although no communication had been allowed among the rabbis.

Another version of the story says that the work was divided among the learned Jews, and that the translation of the prophecies of Isaiah fell to the lot of Simeon. He was very anxious to do the work as well as possible, so that the Greeks might be duly impressed with the beauty and truth of the Jewish Scriptures.

But he soon came to the passage, "Behold, a virgin shall conceive and bear a son, and shall call his name Immanuel." To avoid the mockery of the Greeks, who he knew would point out the absurdity of such a prophecy, Simeon translated the Hebrew term virgin by a Greek word signifying a young woman, and the passage thus rendered could give no cause for cavil.

When he had written it, however, an angel came, effaced the word he had substituted, and replaced it by the proper term. Simeon, undaunted by this correction, and still wishing to avoid giving offence, wrote the translation again and again as he thought it had better be worded. But after the angel had thrice corrected him another miracle occurred, for he suddenly understood that what he had doubted might come to pass. At the same time, a voice warned him that he should not see death until the prophecy had been fulfilled, and the promised Messiah was born.

The translation finished, Simeon returned to Jerusalem, where he dwelt in the Temple, anxiously awaiting the coming Redeemer. Three centuries and more had passed over his head, when Mary entered the sacred precincts to present her Son to the Lord.

As Simeon's eyes fell upon the little group, the Spirit made known to him the divine origin of the Child, whom he took in his arms, exclaiming: " Lord, *now* lettest thou thy servant depart in peace according to thy word: for mine eyes have seen thy salvation, which thou hast prepared before the face of all people ; a light to lighten the Gentiles, and the glory of thy people Israel."

This scene, which is the subject of many a noted picture, is generally called the " Nunc Dimittis." Simeon holds the Infant Saviour in his arms ; Anna the prophetess, stands beside him, and Joseph and Mary are represented listening to his words with awe and wonder. The divine character of the Child is further emphasized in some works of art, by showing Him with the thumb and the first two fingers raised to express the Trinity.

This episode is also, like the circumcision, called the first sorrow of the Virgin, for Simeon, after blessing the little group, addressed Mary, saying: "Behold, this child is set for the fall and rising again of many in Israel; and for a sign which shall be spoken against (yea, a sword shall pierce through thy own soul also); that the thoughts of many hearts may be revealed."

It is in allusion to this text that some artists have depicted Mary with a sword in her heart, and when reference is intended to the seven great sorrows of her life, she is represented pierced by seven swords.

CHAPTER IV.

THE FLIGHT.

Balaam's prophecy — The Magi — The three miracles — The star — Arrival at Jerusalem — Herod and the cock — Adoration of the Magi — Departure of the Magi — Subsequent career of the Magi — The wrath of Herod — The massacre of the Innocents — The flight of Elizabeth — The murder of Zacharias — Joseph warned — The flight into Egypt — The wheat field — The pine and juniper — The roses of Jericho — The aspen — The wild beasts.

THE next momentous event in the Life of Our Lord, according to both Scripture and tradition, is the Adoration of the Magi, so briefly related by Saint Matthew, and so marvelously enlarged by the legends, which alone concern us here.

One version relates that Seth, son of Adam, taught by the angels, foretold the appearance of the Nativity star. This prophecy, repeated much against his will by Balaam (who is identified with Zoroaster), when he would fain have cursed the Lord's chosen people, was: " I shall see him, but not now; I shall behold him, but not nigh ; there shall come a Star out of Jacob, and a sceptre shall rise out of Israel."

Overheard by the Gentiles of the country, Balaam's prediction was believed by them, and repeated to their descendants, who kept up a perpetual watch for the appearance of the miraculous star. Many years had gone by, but their faith remained unshaken, and they still continued to scan the heavens.

Several miracles which occurred to three of their number made the princes, or Magi, as they are generally called, suspect that the time for the fulfilment of the prophecy was very near. One of them saw an ostrich hatch an egg, out of which came a lion, or a wolf, and lamb, which seemed a direct confirmation of Isaiah's words : "the wolf and the lamb shall feed together." The second prince beheld a flower far more beautiful than a rose, and growing upon a vine. As he gazed upon it in admiration, a dove flew out of it, and foretold the birth of Christ. The third of the Magi had a child born to him, and the new-born babe predicted the birth and death of the Redeemer, and died at the end of thirty-three days. The days of the infant's life are supposed to correspond in number with the years which our Lord spent upon earth, although some legends claim that He died at fifty, after having finished his allotted half century of human existence.

Such miraculous portents might well have prepared the minds of the expectant Magi for some unusual event. So all three went up on Mons Victorialis, whence they anxiously began to scan the heavens in search of the long promised sign.

All at once they saw a brilliant star, which far outshone all the rest. As they gazed upon it, it assumed the form of a little child, and moving westward seemed to beckon them on. With loud rejoicings the Magi mounted their waiting dromedaries, and following the beacon star, journeyed straight on to Jerusalem. They arrived in this city at the end of thirteen days, and eagerly began asking every one they met: "Where is he that is born King of the Jews? for we have seen his star in the east and are come to worship him."

> "A star, not seen before, in heaven appearing
> Guided the wise men thither from the east,
> To honour thee with incense, myrrh, and gold;
> By whose bright course led on they found the place,
> Affirming it thy star, new-graven in heaven,
> By which they knew the King of Israel born."
> MILTON: *Paradise Regained.*

Another tradition says that the three wise men were representatives of the three great races descended from Noah's sons, and that starting from different points, and following the guiding star, they met near the gate of Jerusalem, and only then learned that they were all bent on the same quest. On account of this belief, and because they were also supposed to represent the three stages of manhood, the first, Caspar or Jasper, is generally represented as a very old man, with a long white beard and with a Japhetic cast of features. The second, Balthazar, is middle-aged and black-haired, and evidently belongs to a Semitic race; while the third, Melchior, is very young. He is represented either as a Moor or negro, or is attended by a swarthy slave to designate his belonging to the third, or Hametic race, and to show that all the Gentiles also were to have a share in the promised redemption.

The phenomenon in the heavens which so excited the wonder of the Magi has been ascribed by modern science to one of the rarest celestial events. Astronomers tell us that once in about every eight hundred years there is a conjunction of the planets Jupiter and Saturn. Kepler observed this conjunction in 1604, and then noticed a brilliant, but evanescent star.

We are further told that this phenomenon occurred three times in 747 A. U. C., shortly before the birth of Christ, and again the year after with the addition of Mars. These may have been the three suns, which, as we have seen, were reported in the East, where it is well known that astronomy was even then a favourite study.

The state and number of the Magi, and their eager questions, seem to have occasioned quite a sensation in Jerusalem. The rumour of their arrival even reached Herod in his palace. So he sent for the strangers, who, in answer to his questions, told him of the star which they had seen and followed, and of the royal babe whom they had come to worship.

> "And by the light of that same Star
> Three wise men came from country far;
> To seek for a king was their intent,
> And to follow the star wherever it went."
> *Sandy's Christmas Carol.*

A very old ballad or carol, which embodies one of the legends current on this subject during the Middle Ages, tells us that Herod was sitting at table when he heard this news, and vowed that he would not believe it until the roasted cock before him crowed thrice. This quaint production runs thus: —

> "There was a star in the west land
> Which shed a cheerful ray
> Into King Herod's chamber,
> And where King Herod lay.
>
> "The wise men soon espied it,
> And told the king on high, —
> A princely babe was born that night
> No king should e'er destroy.
>
> "'If this be true,' King Herod said,
> 'As thou tellest unto me,
> This roasted cock that lies in the dish
> Shall crow full fences three.'
>
> "The cock soon freshly feathered was
> By the work of God's own hand,
> And then three fences crowed he
> In the dish where he did stand."
>
> *Carnal and Crane.*

The Scriptures relate that Herod was so troubled by the question of the Magi, that he assembled the priests and scribes, who told him that Christ was to be born in Bethlehem of Judea. The legends add that the priests, too, had seen the star, and that they confessed to Herod that the time had come when all their prophecies should be fulfilled.

The wise men, having thus obtained the information they wanted, took leave of Herod, who, pretending that he too was anxious to see and worship the Child heralded by such a miracle, dismissed them saying: "Go and search diligently for the young child, and when ye have found him bring me word again, that I may come and worship him also."

Still following the star, the Magi came to Bethlehem, where their arrival again created a great excitement, and when the star stopped above the stable they eagerly asked if there was a new-born child in the place. Upon receiving an affirmative answer, they quickly dismounted, to do homage to Him whom they had travelled so far to see.

Some versions say that the star waited until the Magi's visit was ended, and then guided them safely home again; but others state that as the wise men entered the stable, it dropped into a well at Bethlehem, at the bottom of which it can still be seen. But if several people try to obtain a glimpse of it at once, it only becomes apparent to the wisest among them.

The Three Kings, having come to do homage to the Lord, brought with them offerings suitable for a king, and thus fulfilled the prophecy: "The kings of Tarshish and the isles shall bring

ADORATION OF THE KINGS. (PFANNSCHMIDT.)

presents, and the kings of Sheba shall offer gifts." These presents are briefly mentioned in Scriptures, but the legends like to expatiate upon the beauty and nature of the gifts, about which they do not always agree. Some versions insist that each one of the kings gave gold as a mark of tribute from a subject to a monarch. Most of them, however, claim that Melchior offered a crown and thirty pieces of gold. The latter were traditional coin, for, made by Terah, father of Abraham, they had been given to the Egyptians in exchange for spices to embalm the body of Jacob. These same coins, which numbered thirty, were subsequently brought by the Queen of Sheba to Solomon, and after passing through many hands were now offered in tribute to his descendant, the long promised and expected Messiah.

The two other kings proffered myrrh and frankincense upon humbly bended knees. These three gifts have ever been considered emblematical of the three-fold nature of Christ. The gold was for the King, the frankincense for the God, and the myrrh for the Man, whose perishable body it was destined to embalm.

The Infant Saviour is frequently represented as receiving these gifts with gracious condescension, and some writers claim that He bestowed upon the givers, in exchange for the gold, incense, and myrrh, the spiritual blessings of love, meekness, and perfect faith.

> " The Magi of the East, in sandals worn,
> Knelt reverent, sweeping round,
> With long, pale beards, their gifts upon the ground,
> The incense, myrrh, and gold
> These baby hands were impotent to hold."
>
> E. B. BROWNING.

The legends assure us that the Magi also offered gifts to Joseph and Mary, and the latter, in return, gave them one of the bands in which the Infant Saviour had been wrapped. Then, after having been warned in a dream not to go back to Jerusalem, where Herod was awaiting their coming only to harm the young king, the Magi took leave of the Holy Family and went home by another way.

Some writers claim that they went to Tarshish, whence they sailed away upon one of the swiftest vessels. But when Herod discovered that they had escaped from him thus, without giving him the required information, he was so angry that he ordered a general destruction of all the vessels in the harbour.

The Magi had effected their escape none too soon. Thanks to the warning they had miraculously received, they reached their own country safely, and proclaimed what they had seen, exhibiting the band which Mary had given them as proof of their words. One of them even ventured to fling the bit of linen into the fire, where it was not consumed, but whence he drew it out unharmed.

To emulate the king whom they had found in a manger, the Magi now gave away all their wealth to the poor, laid aside their rich robes, and went about preaching repentance and doing good. Some forty years later, we are told that the apostle St. Thomas found these men in India, where, after baptizing and instructing them, he bade them continue their good work.

Full of zeal for the Master whom they had seen when a babe lying upon His mother's bosom, the Magi now travelled on into the far East, where they were eventually sentenced to death and perished martyrs of their faith. Their remains, discovered long after, were conveyed by the empress Helena to Constantinople. Frederick Barbarossa, emperor of Germany, transported them next to Cologne, where their bones now rest in a magnificent tomb. Such is the fame of these relics that they have been the object of pious pilgrimages ever since the time of the first crusade, and the shrine of the Magi, or the Three Kings of Cologne, is known throughout all Europe.

Ever since the ninth century a festival has been held in their honour, which is celebrated on the sixth of January, and is known as Epiphany, Twelfth Night, or the Day of the Three Kings. It is marked by popular games and rejoicings, one custom being to elect as king of revels, the person who secures a bean baked in a special cake for that occasion.

> "This is our merry night
> Of choosing king and queen."
> BLACK LETTER:
> *Christmas Carol in the Bodleian Library.*

Other legends state that Herod in the mean time had been vainly awaiting the return of the Magi. When he ascertained that they had really left the country, he flew into one of the awful paroxysms of rage for which he is so famous in history. This tyrant, who in anger once ordered the murder of his beloved wife Mariamne, and of two of his own sons, did not shrink from the massacre of all the children under two years of age, which were found in Bethlehem, and the region round about it.

The Scriptures give no description of this massacre, but the legends dwell upon it at some length. One version relates that Herod sent for the babes, whose mothers hastened to his palace little suspecting why their presence there was required. Then, when the mothers had all been penned into an inner court, from whence there was no possible means of escape, rude soldiers were turned in among them. These men snatched the babes from the arms of the frantic women and butchered them there in cold blood.

Another version describes the troops unexpectedly entering the peaceful village of Bethlehem, and falling upon, and murdering the little ones whom the mothers vainly strove to save. The number of these infant martyrs, who are called the Holy Innocents, is unknown, and has been variously estimated from half a dozen to several thousand. It is hardly likely, however, that in so small a place there should have been more than a score of children under two years of age, and hence they are generally represented as a dozen or more in works of art. As the Holy Innocents died for Christ's sake, they are called the first Christian martyrs, and are often represented as cherubic angels hovering over their Master during His early childhood or at the time of His crucifixion.

> " Who are these on golden wings,
>   That hover o'er the new-born King of Kings,
>   Their palms and garlands telling plain
>   That they are of the glorious martyr train
>   Next to yourself ordained to praise
>   His name, and brighten as on Him they gaze."
>   *Christian Year.*

According to one very old tradition, Elizabeth was then in Bethlehem, with the infant St. John. As the soldiers came to snatch him from her arms, she fled in terror. Closely pursued, and despairing of saving her child, Elizabeth rushed toward a rock, crying frantically, " Mount of God, receive a mother and her child." At these words, the mountain or rock opened wide to receive her, closing again as soon as she was safe within, so that her pursuers could not get at her. Here, in the bosom of the earth, and cheered by a divine light which shone as long as she was forced to remain in hiding, Elizabeth nursed the Precursor, who had been saved by miracle, only that he might prepare the way for the Lord.

Some writers claim that the mountain which opened to receive Elizabeth was transparent, and that Herod's guards could clearly see both mother and child; but others aver that the soldiers did not know what had become of the fugitives, and suspected Zacharias of having concealed them. They made this report to Herod, who, finding that Zacharias could not, or would not reveal the hiding-place of his wife and son, ordered him to be slain between the steps and the altar.

The Levites, entering the temple on the next day, saw the blood-stained altar, and vainly tried to remove all traces of the crime. But one dark spot could not be cleansed; the blood there was congealed, and as if petrified, and a voice was heard proclaiming that all attempts to remove it would be vain until the avenger came.

Terrified by these words, and by the groaning of the wainscoting of the temple, which cried aloud and uttered awful denunciations against Herod, the Levites fled. But ever since then has existed the widespread belief that blood shed by violence cannot be effaced, but leaves an indelible stain. It is owing to this superstition that many dark spots are still pointed out to tourists, in the places where historical crimes have been committed.

As Zacharias was dead, another priest had to be chosen in his stead. This selection, made by casting lots as usual, fell upon Simeon, and a prophetic voice was heard, saying that the newly elected priest should not see death until he had seen the Messiah in the flesh.

The Massacre of the Innocents had been all in vain. Herod had failed to kill the babe he feared, for Joseph, warned by an angel in a dream, had taken Mary and the Child and left Bethlehem in haste. The brevity of the Scriptural narrative, where St. Matthew alone mentions the flight, again contrasts greatly with the legendary accounts, which are as numerous as contradictory.

Some versions say that the Holy Family fled alone, Mary riding upon an ass, and holding the Child, which is always represented as being less than two years old. Other accounts, of which the painters have taken advantage when several figures are desired, say that Joseph was accompanied by his three sons, while Mary was attended by Salome, the girl or woman whose paralysed hand had been restored by touching the Holy Child. The little band is sometimes led or accompanied by angels, either the Holy Innocents, or those who bore witness to the birth of the Redeemer of mankind.

The ass, which Mary rides, is said to have been the same which bent an adoring knee when the Child was laid in the manger, and sometimes the ox is also seen, drawing a rude cart containing the baggage of the Holy Family. As guardian and protector of the Virgin and Child,

Joseph is always present in pictures of the Flight, and while he is sometimes represented as very old, and requiring support from Mary rather than helping her, he is generally a man of middle age, tenderly watchful of his precious charges.

Bethlehem was only two hours' journey from Jerusalem, and from thence to the Egyptian frontier, whither he was divinely ordered to direct his steps, Joseph knew that there was quite a long journey. The time required to cover this distance has been variously estimated as from three days to six months. Some of the legends, however, state that the way was miraculously shortened, and that a few hours after leaving Bethlehem, Joseph, looking up, saw with astonishment the first Egyptian city. We are also told that the Holy Family were led by angels, who pitched a tent for them every night, ferried them over the streams, lulled the Child to sleep by their heavenly strains, and carried a torch or lantern to light the way when they travelled by night.

During the first part of the journey, which took place at night or in the early dawn, Joseph, afraid of pursuit, continually turned his head toward Bethlehem, where some legends say that a signal fire was lighted as soon as the escape of the Holy Family was discovered. The danger of being overtaken was imminent. Mary saw a husbandman sowing grain before sunrise, and hoping to save her Child, she bade the farmer answer, if any one inquired whether an old man, a young woman, and a child had passed by, "Such persons passed this way when I was sowing this corn." The man promised to do as Mary wished, and went home to breakfast.

A few hours later, when the husbandman came to inspect his work, he found that the wheat had grown up by miracle, had ripened, and was ready to harvest. He therefore immediately began to reap it, and when Herod's guards came dashing up, and eagerly inquired whether he had seen the fugitives, he carefully answered as Mary had requested.

> "After that came King Herod,
> With his train so furiously,
> Enquiring of the husbandman
> Whether Jesus passed by this way.
>
> "'Why the truth it must be spoken,
> And the truth it must be known,
> For Jesus passed by this way
> When I my seed had sown.
>
> "'But now I have it reapen,
> And some laid on my wain,
> Ready to fetch and carry
> Into my barn again.'"
>
> Carnal and Crane.

This answer, which was perfectly truthful, — for, as the legend takes care to point out, Mary was far too good to save her Child at the cost of a lie, — put the soldiers off the track. They hastily turned back, although an officious black beetle anxiously pushed itself up out of the brown earth, and chirped, "Last night! last night!"

Since then, the Highlanders, who relate this legend, and consider the beetle a traitor, always stamp upon it, crying, "Last night," to remind the insect that it incurred death in punishment for its intended betrayal. It is in allusion to this legend that a field of ripe grain, where the harvesters are hard at work, is sometimes introduced in the background of pictures representing the Flight into Egypt.

Another legend states that Herod's officers pursued Mary and the Child, and would have overtaken them had not a juniper opened to conceal them, or a pine hidden them beneath its sheltering branches. Most of the plants are said to have remained motionless on this occasion, lest by an inadvertent movement they should reveal the hiding-place of the Lord; but "the brooms and the chick peas rustled and crackled, and the flax bristled up."

> "So Herod was deceived
> By the work of God's own hand,
> And further he proceeded
> Into the Holy Land."
>
> *Carnal and Crane.*

Had Herod only known it, the Child he sought could easily have been traced, for we are told that the Rose of Jericho, which is also called Mary's Rose, sprang up along the path the Holy Family had trodden, and blossomed brightly wherever they rested.

> "And dry Roses bloomed
> Back into beauty, when their garments brushed
> The Rose-bush."
>
> Sir EDWIN ARNOLD: *The Light of the World.*[1]

This flower, which bloomed at the birth of Christ, further showed its sympathy by closing at His crucifixion, only to open again at His resurrection.

Further on, the Holy Family passed into the dense shade of a forest, where they would have lost their way had not an angel guided them. The trees, conscious of the presence of the Creator of the World, are said to have bowed down at His approach and to have done Him obeisance, as was due to a king.

[1] Funk and Wagnall.

> "Once, as Our Saviour walked with men below
> His path of mercy through a forest lay;
> And mark how all the drooping branches show
> What homage best a silent tree may pay." [1]

Only one among them all, the haughty aspen, stood erect, and refused the homage which all the rest were so anxious to bestow. The Infant Saviour, who, according to the Arabic legends, talked even in His cradle, saw the aspen, and solemnly cursed it on account of its pride. Struck to the heart by the sound of his condemnatory words, the guilty tree began to tremble, and has never ceased to shiver since.

> "Only the aspen stood erect and free,
> Scorning to join the voiceless worship pure;
> But see! He cast one look upon the tree,
> Struck to the heart she trembles evermore." [1]

Next the Holy Family came to a cave in the desert, and the youths and Salome going ahead, soon ran back showing signs of the liveliest terror. Their fright was well founded, for out of the cave came lions, dragons, and all manner of wild beasts, ready to devour them. But the Infant Saviour got down from His mother's lap, and went and stood fearlessly among them, while the animals all came and adored Him. Joseph

---

[1] Dyer's Folk Lore of Plants. Appleton & Co.

and Mary were terrified, and trembled; but the Child soon quieted their apprehensions by saying: "Fear not, nor consider me because I am a little infant, for I was and am ever perfect; it must needs be that all the wild beasts of the wood should grow tame before me."

This legend owes its existence to a passage in Isaiah, where the prophet says, "The wolf also shall dwell with the lamb, and the leopard shall lie down with the kid; and the calf and the young lion and the fatling together, and a young child shall lead them." It was completed by making the wild beasts all act as a body-guard to the Holy Family and escort them to Egypt, without molesting the ox, the ass, or the sheep, which formed part of the train.

The desire of giving a Christian meaning to everything, which was a characteristic feature of mediæval literature, made ancient writers add that the Christ Child sprang upon the lion, who, thus honoured above all the rest of the animals, has ever since been termed King of the Animals.

> "First came the lovely lion,
> Which Jesu's grace did spring;
> And of the wild beasts of the field,
> The lion shall be king."
>
> *Carnal and Crane.*

CHAPTER V.

THE SOJOURN IN EGYPT.

The road followed — The brigands — The captives released — The good thief — The robbers' den — The palm — The fountain — The arrival in Egypt — The fallen idols — The conversion of the Egyptians — The priest's son — The Sphinx — The visit to Pharaoh — The dumb bride — The leper girl — The story of the mule — The sojourn at Matarea — The sycamore — The shadow of the cross — Miraculous cures — Bartholomew — Judas — The fortune teller — Christ's playmates — The dead fish — The Egyptian teacher.

SOME commentators tell us that the road followed by the Holy Family led first to Joppa, and then along the coast to Egypt. It was so long and wearisome that Mary's saddle-girth broke on the way. Then, too, as the country was at that time infested with robbers, the travellers, being alone and unarmed, were exposed to many dangers.

One legend relates that a band of brigands, having already secured many captives and much plunder, was lying in wait by the roadside ready to pounce upon the unwary traveller whose coming could be heard from afar. A turn of the road, however, prevented their seeing the approach of the Holy Family. Instead of the tramp of a single ass, the sound of many horses and chariots suddenly fell upon the brigands' ears, and made them flee in haste, leaving their captives and spoil behind them.

The clatter was such, that the captives, too, were terrified and fell upon their faces. When Joseph, Mary, and the Child came into sight, the prisoners slowly rose inquiring in awestruck tones, " Where is the king?" And when Joseph had freed them from their bonds, they went along their way, rejoicing in their miraculous deliverance, and bearing off in triumph the spoil of the brigands.

Another encounter with thieves took place near Ramla, at a spot which is still pointed out to travellers. Here two brigands, who, according to varying versions of the tale are called Dysmas, Demas, Titus, or Matha ; and Gestas, Dumachus, or Joca, were lurking by the roadside. They too wanted to despoil travellers, but as Mary came into sight, one of them, Dysmas — the good thief as the legend calls him — was struck with sudden compassion and begged his companion to let them pass unmolested.

The hard-hearted Gestas insisted however upon accomplishing his proposed theft, and it was only by promising him a girdle and forty pieces of silver, that Dysmas succeeded in bribing him to do the Holy Family no harm. Just as he had succeeded in restraining Gestas, Mary came up, and knowing by intuition all that had happened, she smiled gently upon the good thief, and said to him: "The Lord God will receive thee to His right hand and grant thee the pardon of thy sins."

Another version of this tale states that Mary blessed the merciful thief, and that Christ spoke to him, foretelling the crucifixion about thirty years later, and promising him then the reward of his present good deed. This prediction came true, for the two thieves, crucified on the right and left of the Redeemer, were the self-same men who would fain have waylaid Him. The merciful robber was the one who obtained the promise of being with Christ that day in Paradise.

A third legend of robbers which is sometimes merged into the former, relates that the Holy Family fell into the hands of a gang of thieves, but that the leader was touched by the helplessness of the divine babe, and the purity and gentleness of the young mother. He therefore brought them carefully to his own stronghold in the mountains, where he and his wife ministered unto them.

> " Robbers by the road flung spear and sword
> Down on the sand, and laid their fierce brow there,
> Convinced of evil by mere majesty
> Of Babe and Mother."
>
> Sir EDWIN ARNOLD: *The Light of the World.*[1]

The woman brought water, and helped Mary bathe the Infant Saviour. This water she prudently saved, and when her husband was wounded, some time after the Holy Family left them, she used it to bathe his wound and he was miraculously healed. This is only the first of an endless series of legends, where the water in which the Christ Child was bathed served to cure people of blindness, leprosy, and all manner of illness.

Some learned commentators argue that it is not at all improbable that the Holy Family met the bands of thieves who roamed all over the country at that time, and long after. They add that Mary and her Son escaped unharmed because their helplessness could not but appeal even to such rough men, but the remainder of the tale is, of course, purely mythical, although very poetical.

[1] Funk and Wagnall.

FLIGHT INTO EGYPT. (Van Dyck.)

A favourite legend, especially among artists, to whom it affords a lovely subject for a picture, is that of the palm tree, an episode of the journey to Egypt. Weary and warm, Mary once descended from her patient ass, and sought refuge with her Child beneath a solitary palm. The tall stem of the tree, crowned with its tuft of foliage, afforded her very little shade until the Christ Child bade it move its branches so as to overshadow His mother.

Another much more elaborate version, related in the apocryphal gospels, runs as follows: "And when the blessed Mary had sat down there, she looked at the foliage of the palm and saw it full of fruit, and she said to Joseph, I desire that I may be able to partake of the fruit of this palm." Joseph gazed doubtfully at the tall straight stem, and although anxious to gratify her every wish, he felt too weary and old to attempt to climb the tree. So he told Mary that he felt no craving for the tempting fruit hanging overhead, but longed for a spring of water where he might renew their scanty supply which was almost exhausted. The Christ Child, seeing Mary's evident disappointment, now spoke to the palm-tree, saying: " O tree, bend down thy branches, and with thy fruit refresh my mother." At these words the lofty tree bent down, so that Mary could pluck the fruit hidden among its leaves, and it remained in this humble position until Jesus cried: " Raise thee, O palm, and be strong."

Then, mindful of Joseph's wants also, the Infant Saviour slipped down from His mother's lap, and, thrusting a tiny finger into the dry sand, He bade the water spring out to refresh them. A fountain gushed forth, and there was water in abundance for them all, as well as for the patient ox and ass which accompanied them.

The Holy Family tarried under the palm-tree that night, and on the next morning, when about to depart, the Saviour, anxious to bestow some reward for its good offices, said, " This privilege I grant thee, O palm, that one of thy branches shall be taken by my angels, and planted in the Paradise of my Father. And this blessing I will confer upon thee, that unto all who have conquered in any contest it may be said, Ye have attained the palm of victory."

These words were scarcely finished, when, in the presence of them all, the sky opened and an angel came floating down from heaven to do His bidding. Plucking a branch from the top of the tree, the angel winged its way back to Paradise, to plant it there by the River of Life, where it would flourish forever.

Needless to state there is a very obvious anachronism in this legend, for the palm had long been considered an emblem of victory by the ancients, as can be seen in many anti-Christian writings. This legend was therefore invented, like so many others, merely to give a Christian signification to an old heathen symbol, which it was neither possible nor advisable to do away with entirely. In early Christian art, the palms brought to the martyrs by angels are, moreover, supposed to be leaves plucked from the miraculously transplanted tree under which Our Lord once found rest.

Shortly after the halt under the obedient palmtree, Joseph, feeling the intense heat sorely, consulted Jesus, — whom many legends make the director of the journey,— and asked Him whether it would not be possible to hold their course along the sea shore where every passing breeze would refresh them ? In answer to this question the Christ Child said : " Fear not, Joseph, I will shorten the way for you, so that what you were to go in the space of thirty days, you shall accomplish in this one day."

These words were soon fulfilled, and before nightfall the Holy Family reached the town of Sotinen on the borders of Hermopolis. As no one came out to offer them hospitality, and as they did not know where else to go to obtain shelter, they soon directed their steps to a sanctuary, " which was called the Capitol of Egypt, in which temple three hundred and fifty-five idols were placed, to which, on separate days, the honour of the Deity was rendered in sacrilegious rites."

To give a literal interpretation to the words of the prophet Isaiah, " and the idols of Egypt shall be moved at his presence," various legends have been invented, which for the greater part resemble one another very closely. The first is that as Mary and the Child set foot in this temple, the three hundred and fifty-five idols fell prostrate and lay upon the floor shattered to pieces.

The crash of the falling images was such, that the people ran and told their ruler, and he hastened to the spot with all his army. When he arrived there all was still, and entering the temple alone, his eyes wandered over the shattered idols. They fell at last upon the divine Child, peacefully slumbering in the arms of His Virgin Mother, who gazed with awe at the ruins around her.

The ruler, impressed by the repose of the Christ Child, passed out of the temple, and after telling the assembled people what he had seen, he added: "If this were not the God of our gods, our gods would by no means have fallen on their faces before him, neither would they lie prostrate in his sight; wherefore, they silently avow him to be the Lord. We then, if we do not very carefully what we see our gods do, may incur the peril of his indignation, and may come to destruction, as befell Pharaoh, king of the Egyptians; who, not believing such great miracles, was drowned with all his army in the sea." Thus adjured, the Egyptians believed in Christ, and did homage to Him.

Another version of this legend relates that, as the Holy Family entered the temple at On, there was a great earthquake, and the statue of Ra, the Egyptian god, fell prostrate at their feet.

> "And coming nigh to On,
> Where stands the house of Ra, its mighty God,
> Cut in black porphyry, prodigious, feared, —
> Fell from his seat."
> Sir EDWIN ARNOLD: *The Light of the World.*[1]

In another place, the idols themselves are said to have testified to the divinity of the Child who was about to come among them, for when they were questioned by their priests as usual, they said: "There cometh hither a God in secret,

[1] Funk and Wagnall.

who surely is a God, neither is any God beside him worthy of worship, because he is truly the Son of God." Then, their reign being ended, these idols fell, and the people worshipped the Christ.

The Holy Family was once resting in a hospital, in one of these heathen cities, and Mary took advantage of the halt to wash the swaddling clothes of the Child which she spread out upon some wood to dry. The son of a neighbouring priest, a demoniac, mischievously snatched one of these cloths as he was passing by and put it upon his head. At the same moment, "the demons began to come forth out of his mouth, and fled in the form of crows and serpents." Then, while the witnesses stood there aghast, Jesus spoke to the child, and he was healed, to the great joy of his father. When the latter heard exactly how the miraculous cure had been effected, he gave thanks to God, and he also testified to the divinity of the babe by whose agency the cure had been effected.

The falling of the Egyptian idols has been the subject of many a picture, and while the old masters have as a rule represented the occurrence realistically, modern painters have preferred to turn the episode into an allegory. In some pictures they show us the Virgin calmly nursing her

REPOSE IN EGYPT. (MERSON.)

Child beneath the huge image of Isis and her son Horus,—idols whose power was indeed at an end, although they did not fall into dust at the Redeemer's appearance.

One modern picture, which exercises a great fascination upon all who have seen it, shews us the Virgin and Child calmly sleeping between the great paws of the crouching Sphinx. The mysterious riddle is thus solved by the nimbus around the Christ-Child, and this light, with the dim glow of the stars and the flicker of a smouldering fire, alone illumines the peaceful scene.

Some of the legends inform us that the Holy Family journeyed to Memphis, where they were received by Pharaoh (although there were no Pharaohs left in those days), and remained there three years. Other very extraordinary stories, which by their resemblance to the tales of the Thousand and One Nights betray their Arabian origin, are also related in connection with the sojourn of the Holy Family in Egypt.

We are told, for instance, that they once saw a demoniac woman, who, in spite of all the restraints placed upon her by friends and relatives, always managed to escape from them and run about naked at night. Mary gazed compassionately upon this unfortunate creature, and cured her by that one kind look.

A little further on they came to a town, where the family which entertained them was in deep sorrow. Upon inquiring the cause of their grief, Mary learned that the daughter, a bride, had been struck dumb by enchantment. But when the bride had touched the Infant Saviour, as Mary bade her, the spell was broken and she spoke, returning thanks for her miraculous cure.

Another woman, also a demoniac, craved permission to hold the heavenly Child, and was immediately restored to her right mind. In her joy and gratitude she begged the travellers to come and rest in her house, where she eagerly brought perfumed water to bathe Christ. When the bath was finished, the woman sprinkled a few drops of this water upon a leper girl, who was cured by the contact. In her intense gratitude this maiden followed the Holy Family during the remainder of their journey.

Their next resting place was at the house of a prince. There, too, sadness prevailed; but it was only after great persuasions that the princess confided to the girl the cause of her grief, and told her that her only son, a child of four years of age, was a leper. As soon as the girl heard this she eagerly related her own marvellous cure, and the noble mother, in obedience to her instructions, plunged her suffering child into the water which Mary had used to bathe her Son, and the lad was immediately restored.

In another house where they rested, a husband and wife were estranged; but in the presence of the Redeemer no division could endure, and the couple henceforth lived in perfect unity and joy, while the Holy Family wandered on, leaving only blessings in its wake.

As they entered a certain town, they saw three women, clad in mourning, come weeping out of a cemetery. The leper girl drew near them to ask where her party could find shelter, and the women, notwithstanding their grief, invited the travellers into their own house, and provided all that was necessary for their comfort.

The former leper girl vainly tried to discover the cause of their grief; but when she saw them enter a special chamber, and, falling upon the neck of a mule which was kept there, kiss it with many tears and words of endearment, she could no longer restrain her curiosity, and asked them what all this meant. Still weeping copiously, the women told her that the mule was their only and beloved brother. He had been changed into a beast by magic arts on the eve of his wedding, and although they had tried every form of exorcism, they had not been able to break the spell and restore him to his wonted shape.

After again relating her own experiences, the leper persuaded the women to come and consult the Virgin Mary, telling them she would be sure to find some way to help them. Mary, having heard their pitiful tale, "lifted up the Lord Jesus and put him on the back of the mule, and herself wept along with the women; and to Jesus Christ she said, 'Alas! my son; heal this mule by thy great power, and make him a man endued with reason as he was formerly.' When these words proceeded from the mouth of my lady, Lady Mary, the mule changed its form, and became a man, a young man, who was whole, without any blemish. Then he and his mother and his sisters adored my lady, Lady Mary, and began to kiss the Child, holding him above their heads, saying, 'Blessed is thy mother, O Jesus, O Saviour of the world; blessed are the eyes which enjoy the happiness of beholding thee.'"

As the ex-leper girl had been the agent in bringing about this marvelous cure, the grateful family now proposed that she should marry the restored heir, and the wedding was celebrated with feast and dancing and song, for the house of mourning had been turned into a place of rejoicing. The only tears shed were when Mary and the Christ Child departed, for these happy people could not bear to lose sight of the Holy Family, which had turned their weeping into joy.

The travellers came at last to a sycamore, which some authorities say grew in the Thebaid, a place which hence became the favourite resort of many anchorites during the first centuries of our era. Other versions, however, state that the sycamore stood at Matarea, near Cairo, where it can still be seen, for although it was cut down by the Saracens, it again sprang up from its roots with renewed vigour.

The Holy Family pitched their tent under this sycamore, which moved its branches from sunrise to sunset in order to afford them constant protection from the burning Egyptian sun.

> "And a way-side sycamore
> Beneath whose leaves they rested, moved his boughs
> From noon till evening with the moving sun
> To make them shade."
>
> Sir EDWIN ARNOLD: *Light of the World*.[1]

As there was no water here to refresh them, a fountain sprang up at a word from the Christ

---

[1] Funk and Wagnall.

Child, or, according to another legend, the fountain of bitter water which flowed there so freely, became wholesome and sweet for their use.

The Holy Family dwelt here for a period of time which has been variously estimated as from one to seven years. Mary tended her Child, washing His garments in the fountain, and spreading them out to dry upon the surrounding bushes which blossomed spontaneously at their touch. The Holy Family, according to some legends, was quite well-to-do, owing to the gifts of the Wise Men, and the contributions of the wealthy, whom the Christ Child or His mother healed. Other writers relate that they were extremely poor, and were entirely dependent upon the exertions of Joseph, whose skill as a carpenter was not very great.

Such was their poverty, that Mary went from door to door, begging a little fine flax, until she had collected enough to make the first garment which her Son wore, when old enough to be taken out of the usual swaddling bands. To eke out their small income, Mary laboured diligently, and in pictures representing her at this time she is always spinning, if not busy with household tasks, or in caring for her Child.

Some legends state that it was here, under the Egyptian sycamore, which is known as the Virgin's tree, that the Infant Saviour took His first steps. It was at sundown, and as He tottered toward his mother's outstretched arms, His shadow fell upon the yellow sand, forming a distinct and prophetic cross.

During their sojourn there, Mary effected many miraculous cures, generally by bathing the affected parts of the sufferers in the same water in which she had washed her Child. Sometimes, sick children recovered as soon as they were laid in her arms, and hence many people suppose that the Infant in the arms of Holbein's celebrated Mayer Madonna, is not her own child, but one whom the Virgin has been implored to save from death or disease.

A mother in the neighbourhood of Matarea had two children who sickened at the same time. One of them died and was buried, and then the other became so very ill that the mother saw she would lose it too. As a last hope of saving her child, she took it in her arms and carried it to Mary, whose help she anxiously besought.

Gazing upon the sick child, Mary saw that it had died on the way; but she made no sign and only bade the woman lay her babe in the cradle beside the sleeping Jesus. The woman did so, and when the dead child came into contact with the Redeemer, he was restored to life and perfect health. The legends add that his name was Bartholomew, and that he became one of the twelve disciples who followed Our Lord during His short time of ministry upon earth.

Mary Cleopas, whom some writers claim as an elder half-sister of Mary the Virgin, dwelt not far from there with her husband and child. Her life was not happy, for in the same house dwelt her rival who had a child of the same age as hers. Both children sickened, but Mary Cleopas, having wrapped her boy in a garment which had belonged to the Christ Child, saved him, while her rival's son died.

Envious of the happiness of Mary Cleopas in the continued possession of her child, the rival now sought to injure the lad, whom she thrust into a heated oven one day when the mother had been called away for a few minutes. Mary Cleopas returned in haste, and after some search found her child in the oven, not burned to a crisp as her rival expected, but well and comfortable, thanks to the Saviour's garment which he wore beneath his own clothes.

Sometime after this, the envious woman thrust the child into a well, but he floated like a water lily on the surface of the water until rescued from this perilous position. Baffled and angry, the wicked woman stood gazing down into the well and wondering why the child, whom she hated, had not been drowned. Suddenly, she lost her balance, and fell into the water, where she sank like a stone and perished miserably, because she had no magic garment to preserve her like the innocent child.

There are several other cures recorded of the sick and the blind, and many extraordinary cases of the ejection of evil spirits, which in various forms, such as dragons and vampires, tormented unfortunate women. But there is so much similarity about these tales, that they need not be given here at any length, and it will be sufficient to relate the most important, which is as follows : —

A woman, whose son was possessed of an evil spirit, once brought him to Mary, imploring her to cure him. In answer to this appeal, the Infant Saviour stretched out His hand and touched the child, bidding the demon depart. Thus adjured, Satan, in the form of a dog, left the child, throwing him into convulsions. In his writhing the sufferer struck Christ in the side, on the very spot where He received the cruel lance thrust at the time of the Crucifixion.

Such was the pain that the Christ Child felt

that He wept aloud, until His mother comforted Him. Then the grateful woman departed with her son, Judas Iscariot, and he lived to betray the Redeemer who had delivered him in vain from the power of the Evil One.

It was also during that sojourn at Matarea that the Holy Family were visited by a gypsy, who begged to see the palm of the Christ Child. She foretold the salient points of His career, such as His baptism, temptation, ministry, trial, and crucifixion, filling Mary's heart with anguish.

> "Thy Son so well beloved
> Thou once shalt see Him lie,
> Stretched out upon a cross
> To suffer there and die."
>
> *New Ballad of Our Lady.*

This legend, which was very popular in the Middle Ages, and which is preserved in songs which were sung in the sixteenth century, has given rise to several noted pictures, where we see the Christ Child with one or more gypsies. In some versions of the ballad, the gypsy, in exchange for her prophecy, receives the guerdon of true repentance and eternal life; in others several gypsies end by begging a coin to "wet their thirsty throats."

Artists have often used the Repose in Egypt

as theme for their pictures, and examples of this subject are as varied as numerous. Besides sometimes embodying one or more of the legends related above, we often see the Christ Child playing near His mother or Joseph, and frequently He has, as companions or playmates, a host of little child angels, generally supposed to represent the Holy Innocents.

These little cherubs, whom some painters represent more like Cupids than anything else, are often busy playing with the shavings, or picking up chips, and pretending to help Joseph or Mary in their homely avocations. In the background of the picture we often see some scene from the Old Testament, or a foreshadowing of the life which awaited the Redeemer upon earth.

There are a few more legends which properly belong to this epoch. For instance, we are told that "Jesus was three years old, and when He saw boys playing, He began to play with them. And He took a dry fish and put it in a basin, and ordered it to breathe, and it began to breathe. And He said again to the fish: 'Reject the salt which thou hast, and move in the water,' and so it came to pass."

The legends which depict the Christ Child as a healer, comforter, and helper, in that they retain at least a faint sense of His mission upon earth, and show some perception of His character, are, however untrue, still not repulsive, but a legend like the one above quoted, where it is claimed that a miracle was performed as a pastime, shows how ignorant the people must have been who could imagine such a thing in connection with His Name. There are, though, so many legends of this kind, that, however false, puerile, and even at times shocking, they may be, it is impossible to have any idea of the mediæval literature on this subject, unless they are mentioned together with those which are more pleasing.

Thus we are told that as Jesus passed through the streets of a certain city, with Mary His mother, He came upon the market-place, where a teacher was instructing his pupils. The master sat beneath a high wall, and was so absorbed in his teaching that he paid no heed to a nest full of sparrows quarrelling directly over his head, until the birds fell into his lap. Jesus laughed aloud at the master's dismay, and His rude laughter so provoked the teacher's anger that the latter drove him out of the town.

CHAPTER VI.

THE BOYHOOD OF CHRIST.

The return to Nazareth — Christ and St. John — The broken pitcher — The children refuse to play — The story of the kids — The young king — Simon Zelotes — The seven pools — The sparrows — Two boys slain — The wrathful parents — The miracles — The education of Jesus — Zaccheus — Levi — The fruit tree — The roof accident — The dead babe — The sojourn at Jericho — The grain — The lions — The bedstead — The throne — The sojourn at Capernaum — The dead man restored — The sojourn at Bethlehem — James cured — The mason — Christ's home life — The dyer — The twelve year old Christ at Jerusalem.

THE sojourn of the Holy Family in Egypt, whether long or short, was ended by a heavenly warning to Joseph, according to the Scripture narrative, or by an angelic visitation to Mary, as is stated in the legends. The Christ Child was now old enough to walk, and although the return journey must have been performed nearly in the same way as the flight, artists generally represent the Saviour as walking, and sometimes even as leading the ass, or carrying Joseph's bag of tools. The massacre of the

Holy Innocents, which at times is introduced in the background, is here intended to remind the spectator of the cause for the hurried flight from Palestine.

The Holy Family, as we know, had intended to return to Bethlehem, but when Joseph "heard that Archelaus did reign in Judea in the room of his father Herod, he was afraid to go thither; notwithstanding, being warned of God in a dream, he turned aside into the parts of Galilee; and he came and dwelt in a certain city called Nazareth."

This was, as we have seen, the native place of the Virgin Mary, and while some commentators argue that the Holy Family went to dwell in the rather palatial dwelling which she had inherited from her father Joachim, others claim that they lived in one of the rude huts, such as were used in those days by the fisher folk among whom they had come to dwell.

Here, while Joseph plied his trade as a carpenter, and Mary looked after the household, the boy Christ "grew and waxed strong in spirit, filled with wisdom; and the grace of God was upon him." These few words contain all the real information which has been vouchsafed us concerning the boyhood of Our Lord.

This, in some respects, tantalizing brevity

leaves the field open for conjecture ; and while some of us like to imagine the Saviour as spending a beautiful, healthy, and happy childhood, in close communion with nature, quite like all other children except in His perfect sinlessness, the apocryphal and mediæval writers have imagined stories, grave and gay, poetical and puerile, beautiful and malevolent, and have thus tried to complete the biography of Christ. Were it not for the evidently good intentions of those who imagined these tales, and who sinned through ignorance only, many of these stories would be branded as sacrilegious, which, considered from our point of view only, they undoubtedly are.

It has been a much discussed matter whether St. John really was a playmate of Our Lord, as so many artists have taken pleasure in representing him. This can never be positively decided, and as Holy Families often include, besides the Mother and Child, St. John, Elizabeth, Joseph, and Zacharias, we are familiar with the two children in art. Although in some pictures St. John is represented as four or five years older than his Master, he was His senior only by about three months. St. John often holds a cross in his hand, of which the shadow either falls *behind* him, to show that the Crucifixion took place after his death, or directly upon the Christ

Child, who sometimes stretches out His hand for it as if to claim the cross as His own.

The children are seen in art playing together, embracing each other, clinging to the Virgin's knee, gathering flowers, going to school, or running to fetch water from the fountain. One legend relates that the Christ Child, in His hurry to bring water to His mother, once broke His pitcher. Undismayed by this accident, He brought the water home in a corner of His robe, or in the handkerchief which He, like all the people around Him, wore on His head to protect Himself from the too ardent sun.

Another legend tells us that one day Christ ran out in search of playmates. He soon came to a group of merry children, but when He asked them to play with Him they one and all refused, because they had heard rumours of His strange birth, and did not consider Him their equal.

> "He said, 'God bless you every one,
> May Christ your portion be!
> Little children, shall I play with you,
> And you shall play with Me?'
>
> "But they jointly answered 'No;'
> They were lords' and ladies' sons,
> And He, the meanest of them all,
> Was born in an ox's stall."
>
> *The Holy Well.*

Grieved by this refusal, the Christ Child slowly turned away and went home again, while His tears dropped down "like water from the skies." Running into the house, He told the whole story to His mother, who — contrary to her well known gentleness — bade Him make use of His power to destroy the children who had thus slighted Him.

> "Sweet Jesus, go to yonder town,
>   As far as the Holy Well,
> And take away those sinful souls,
> And dip them deep in Hell."
>
> *The Holy Well.*

But this advice was not followed by the Divine Child. He dried His tears, made up His mind to forget the insult, and forgave the children whose refusal to share His games had caused Him such a grievous disappointment.

> "'Nay, nay,' sweet Jesus mildly said,
> 'Nay, nay, that must not be;
>   For there are too many sinful souls
>   Crying out for the help of Me.'"
>
> *The Holy Well.*

On another occasion Jesus went down into the village to play with the boys. As the latter did not wish to share His games, they hid away in the houses, telling their mothers not to reveal their hiding place. The Christ Child soon came to the door of a house where several boys were concealed, and asked the woman who stood on the threshold where her children might be. She promptly answered that she did not know, although the suppressed titter of the children, and their rustling in the straw where they were hiding, were quite audible where she stood. Gazing up into her face in wonder, the Christ Child asked: "What is the noise I hear?" Unabashed by this question, the woman said it was only the kids rustling in the straw. Then Jesus cried aloud: "Come out here, O Kids, to your shepherd." The rustle in the straw became louder, and in a few minutes the woman saw her children rush out into the street in the shape of kids and begin to skip around the Lord. In her terror the mother now besought Christ to forgive the lie she had uttered, and restore her children to their former condition. Ever ready to forgive, the Lord Jesus therefore said: "Come, boys, let us go and play;" and immediately, while the woman stood there, the kids were changed back into boys.

"Now in the month of Adar, Jesus assembled the boys as if He were their king; they strewed their garments on the ground, and He sat upon them. Then they put on His head a crown wreathed of flowers, and like attendants waiting on a king, they stood in order before Him on His right hand and on His left."

> "In month of Adar, Syrian boys
> Playing in Nazareth, — as thou hast seen, —
> With girdled frocks, striped tunics, and feet bare,
> Found Him, and crowned Him with white lily-buds,
> And put a stick of lilies in His hand,
> And set Him on the hillside, bending knee
> In merry worship, and made whoso passed
> Halt and bow lowly, crying: 'Hither come,
> Worship our King, then wend upon thy way.'"
> Sir EDWIN ARNOLD: *Light of the World*.[1]

This pretty picture, which is preserved for us in the Arabic Gospel of the Infancy, has never yet, as far as I am aware, been used by artists, although it is often alluded to by poets. The latter add that the Christ Child held as sceptre a slender reed, a shoot of the flowering almond, a branch of lilies, or a spike of gladiolus.

When all was ready, the boys who acted as ushers forced all those who passed along the road to come and do homage to the king whom they had chosen, before they would allow them to pass along their way. Presently there came two men carrying a boy who seemed dead. This lad had gone into the forest, where, climb-

[1] Funk and Wagnall.

ing a tall tree, he eagerly thrust his hand into a nest to steal the eggs it contained.

But there was a poisonous serpent coiled up in the centre of the nest, and it bit the boy, who had only strength enough left to crawl down from the tree. He lay upon the ground, like one bereft of life, when his relatives came in search of him.

Notwithstanding the evident grief of the bearers, the boys forced them to come and do homage to Jesus. But He, learning the cause of their sorrow, rose from his improvised throne, and bidding them follow Him with the dead, hastened to the spot where the accident had occurred.

Here Jesus, pausing at the foot of the tree, called to the serpent, and at His voice it came forth and did homage to Him. Then Jesus said: "Go and suck out all the venom which thou hast infused in the boy." The serpent obeyed, and when the operation was ended, the Lord cursed the serpent, which was "rent asunder," and stroking the child gently, restored him to life. This boy was, we are told, Simon Zelotes, who eventually became one of Christ's faithful followers.

After a violent rain storm, the child Jesus once went to play near the banks of the Jordan, where He made seven little pools in the mud, and connected them by small channels. Then, displeased with the turbid appearance of the water, He cleared it with a word, and bade it flow back and forth as He pleased.

Fascinated by this sight, the children of the neighbourhood all gathered around Him, and presently all began to fashion animals out of the moist clay. The little ones were delighted with their handiwork, until Jesus showed the superiority of His, by making them alive at a word, or changing them back into mere clay at His will. Last of all, Jesus fashioned twelve clay sparrows, which stood in a row before Him and with which He was greatly pleased.

The children's pastime had not been unnoticed however, and a Pharisee, shocked by such games on a Sabbath-day, went to Joseph and inquired why he allowed the Child Jesus to do that which was not lawful on the Sabbath-day. Joseph hastened to the spot where his foster son was playing, and addressing Jesus reproved Him for not observing the Sabbath-day.

Jesus gazed up at him in wonder for a moment, and then spreading out his hands, He said to the sparrows: " Retire aloft and fly; ye shall find death from no one." At these words the sparrows, or plovers, soared upward, and the Icelandic legend claims that they all chirped *deerrin* or *dyrnhin*, which means "glory," a cry which they have repeated ever since.

> "He made
> Birds out of clay, and clapped His hands, and lo !
> They chirruped, spread their wings, and flew away."
>   Sir EDWIN ARNOLD: *Light of the World.*[1]

The son of Annas, Hanani, or of a devil, as he is variously termed in Apocryphal writings, was standing by with a willow wand. He now maliciously closed all the channels, so that the water could not flow to and fro, or he broke them open and allowed all the moisture to escape.

When Jesus saw this wanton mischief, He was very angry indeed, and cried: " Impious and lawless one, how have the pools offended thee and why hast thou emptied them ? Thou shalt not finish thy journey, and shalt be withered like the stick which thou holdest." This awful curse was soon accomplished, for the child fell down and expired. His terrified playmates then ran to tell his parents, and Joseph, who hastened down to the spot, took the Christ Child by the shoulder, and led Him home. On the way thither, another boy, also "'a worker of in-

---

[1] Funk and Wagnall.

iquity," jostled the Child Jesus so roughly that He turned upon him, saying: "Thou shalt not return whole from the way in which thou goest," and immediately he too fell down and died.

According to one account, Joseph took the Christ Child by the ear and scolded Him roundly; according to another he dared not say a word to Him, but begged Mary to reason with Him and bring Him back to a better state of feelings. While Mary was arguing with Jesus, whom the legends, in their ignorant simplicity, describe as sullen and revengeful, the parents of the dead children came with the corpses, which they laid at Mary's feet, uttering loud complaints and accusations. The Christ Child began by striking His accusers blind; but, relenting after a while, He restored them to sight and brought the children back to life. The apocrypha describes the process of one of these resurrections in these words: "The same hour Jesus took the dead child by the ear, and held him up from the ground in the sight of all; and they saw Jesus talking with him as a father with his son. And his spirit returned into him, and he lived again." The account closes with the appropriate remark, "and they all marvelled," as every one must, at their having dared to imagine such tales in connection with One whose life was full of forgiveness for all those who injured Him, and whom they thus maligned, although they recognized His divinity.

The people were so terrified at the power of the Christ Child, that they implored Joseph and Mary to go away, or to teach the Child to bless, instead of blasting them with terrible curses which took such prompt effect.

Now, while most of the legends say that Jesus must have taken His first lessons at His mother's knee, the apocrypha relates His experience with several school-masters. For instance, we are told in the apocrypha that Jesus was taken first to Zaccheus, where He refused to learn His letters or to repeat the law, saying, " I was before the law, thou shalt be instructed by Me." And then, to the amazement of the teacher, He repeated the letters which He had never learned, and expounded their occult meaning in the following words, which are intentionally unintelligible: " Hear Me, doctor, understand the first letter. Observe how it hath two lines; in the middle, advancing, remaining, giving, scattering, varying, menacing; threefold and doubly mingling; like the mind at the same time having all things common."

The astonishment of the teacher was further increased when this uncanny pupil began to relate how He had seen Abraham and Noah, and that He was born before the world was made. Zaccheus, in a quandary, then implored Joseph to take the Child away, declaring he could teach Him nothing, and saying that he knew not whether the pupil proposed to him was God or an angel. Jesus, angry with this man for having presumed to try and instruct Him, now struck him dead with a word ere He returned home.

Jesus' next teacher, Levi, was much like the first, and when Christ bade him explain the hidden meaning of the letters he pretended to teach, he remained dumb, and threatened his pupil with "a rod of thorax tree." Scorning the threat, Jesus proceeded to give him also an explanation as mysterious as the one quoted above.

Levi, still more amazed than his predecessor, now made a complete apology, and acknowledged the divinity of his Scholar. This recognition of His powers pleased the Christ Child, who proclaimed a general amnesty, saying: "Let the unfruitful be fruitful, and the blind see, and the lame walk well, and the poor enjoy good things, and the dead live again, that in a restored condition every one may return and abide in Him who is the root of life and of perpetual sweetness." At these words, all those who were ill, and all those whom He had stricken with blindness, were restored, and even Zaccheus came back to life.

During the first centuries of Christianity we are told that pilgrims visited the school which Christ attended, saw the A. B. C. book which he had used, and gazed in awe upon a miraculous beam upon which He had once sat. This beam, which could easily be moved by Christians, could not be lifted by Jews or unbelievers, if the account of a sixth century traveller is to be believed.

It was during the sojourn in Nazareth that Christ is said to have created a tree. The fruit which immediately appeared upon it was distributed among His little playmates, who had longed for such a treat, and whose tastes He took pleasure in gratifying.

Once, when a whole troop of children were playing on the usual flat roof of an oriental house, one of their number was accidentally pushed over the low parapet. He fell to the ground, where he lay lifeless, and his terrified playmates fled. Jesus was standing by him when the parents came in haste, and accused Him of having pushed the child over and thus caused his death. Jesus did not reply a word to this storm of accusations, but remained obstinately silent until Mary implored Him to speak and tell them that He was not to blame for the accident.

Turning to the dead child, Christ now addressed him by name, saying, "Zeno! (for so his name was called) rise and tell me; did I cast thee down?" And immediately he rose and said, "Nay, Lord, Thou hast not cast me down, but raised me up." The parents, overjoyed at seeing their child alive once more, and as well as ever, departed, blessing the Lord, who had done such a miracle in their favour.

Some time after, Christ heard a woman wailing over the body of her dead babe. Touched by her sorrow, Jesus laid His hand upon the infant, saying: "I say unto thee, babe, do not die, but be with thy mother;" and the child, restored to health, smiled in its mother's arms.

Although, as we have seen, some of these imaginary miracles were benevolent and in keeping with what we know of Christ's character, the remainder were so uncanny that the people again asked Mary and Joseph to go away, and they went to dwell at Jericho.

Here the Child went out with his foster-father to sow corn; but while Joseph sowed a measure of grain, Jesus sowed one single seed. This, however, grew and multiplied so rapidly that the

Christ Child, having reaped and threshed the grain, " made a hundred quarters of it," which He bestowed upon all the neighbouring poor.

On the road which led from Jericho to the Jordan, there was then a cave where a lioness had taken up her abode with her cubs. This ravenous beast was the terror of the whole country side, and many people lost their lives in trying to pass along the road or to slay her. The Christ Child, who was then only eight years of age, resolved to put an end to this state of affairs, and He marched fearlessly down the road, followed at a safe distance by the awestruck people. They, of course, expected to see the lioness pounce upon Him and tear Him limb from limb; but, to their intense surprise, the wild beasts all fawned upon Him.

While they caressed Him, Christ turned to the wondering people and said, " How much better than you are the beasts, which recognize and glorify their Lord; and ye men, who are made in the image and likeness of God, know Him not. Beasts acknowledge Me, and grow gentle; men see Me, and know Me not."

This speech ended, Christ bade the lions follow Him, and led them down to the Jordan, whose waters parted on the self-same spot where the ark had been carried over in the days of

Joshua so many centuries before. Jesus thus led the lions across the river to the desert, on the other side, where He dismissed them, saying, "Go in peace."

As has already been stated, Joseph was a carpenter. He seems, moreover, to have been a sad bungler at his trade, for in the apocrypha we constantly find him making mistakes, which the Child Jesus rectifies by miracles. With a touch Jesus seems to have filled the edges which refused to meet, and smoothed the rough places. Several anecdotes relating such miracles have been preserved for us. For instance, we hear that Joseph, called upon to make a bedstead for a certain ruler, went with the Child into the forest in search of the necessary timber. When the pieces were ready, Joseph discovered that one was much shorter than the other, and began to bewail his lost labour. But the Christ Child bade him not give way to despair, saying, "Come, let us take hold of the ends of each piece of wood, and lay them together end for end, and let us pull them toward us, for we shall be able to make them equal." Joseph obeyed, and after a little vigorous tugging, the board, miraculously lengthened, was just the right size for the required bedstead.

Shortly after this occurrence, Joseph was

commissioned to make a throne for the king of Jerusalem, and given the exact dimensions of the place it was to occupy. Two whole years of constant labour were spent in carving this throne; but when it was completed it proved too short to fit the required space. Joseph was in despair. Fearing he had lost the proceeds of two whole years of work, he went to bed in sorrow, after refusing to partake of any food. The Christ Child, seeing his evident grief, inquired what caused it, and having learned the whole story, He bade Joseph seize one end of the throne, grasped the other Himself, and pulled until it had stretched to the right length.

As the Christ Child was such an efficient helper, it is no wonder that Joseph took Him with him wherever he went, so that He might remedy his manifold mistakes.

> "Afterwards, people told
> Strange tales of those hid days, — how, at His toil,
> Touching a plank, it stretched to rightful length,
> Or shortened at His will, — the dead wood quick
> To live again and serve Him."
> Sir EDWIN ARNOLD: *Light of the World.*[1]

We next hear of the Holy Family as settled at Capernaum, where a man was taken violently

[1] Funk and Wagnall.

ill and soon died. Hearing the lament for the dead, Christ now bade Joseph take the handkerchief off his own head and lay it upon the face of the corpse, saying, "Christ save thee." Joseph obeyed, and the man was restored to his happy family. It may be this story which gave rise to the mediæval belief in the curative powers of Joseph, as well as of Joachim.

While the Holy Family dwelt for some time at Bethlehem, Joseph sent James out into the garden to gather herbs to make pottage. Jesus accompanied his brother, and was playing near him when He suddenly heard James utter a cry of pain. Looking up, the Christ Child saw that a viper, hidden under the leaves, had bitten James, whose hand was already swelling fast. To spring forward, grasp the injured member, and breathe gently upon it was the work of a moment. As the breath of the Holy Child fell upon his wound, James felt it heal, and when he turned around in search of the viper he saw it dead at his feet.

On another occasion Jesus and James went out into the woods to tie faggots. Here James accidentally cut his foot with the axe, and he would have bled to death had he not been miraculously cured by his little brother. A similar tale is also told of a woodcutter, who, according to some legends, actually died from loss of blood, and was restored to life by the Christ Child.

One day there was a great clamour in the small town where the Holy Family lived, for a man had fallen from a house which he was building and had been killed. Jesus arose and went to the scene of the accident. There He took the dead man by the hand, and cried : " I say unto thee, man, arise, and do thy work." At these words the man arose and after worshipping Him returned to his unfinished labours.

The apocryphal gospels further tell us that whenever Joseph and Mary made a feast, none of their guests dared touch the food until the Holy Child had broken and blessed it and partaken of it first. If at any time He refused to come to His meals, the family could not eat, and all fasted as long as He was not there to share the food with them. Thus, His relatives, " having His life before their eyes as a light, regarded and feared Him. And when Jesus slept, whether by day or by night, the brightness of God shone on Him."

Many writers claim that Jesus' " brethren," as they are called in the Scriptures, were not Joseph's sons by a previous marriage, but rather his nephews. Other authorities state that they were related to Our Lord through His mother, because Anna, the wife of Joachim, either before she married this worthy, or after his death, had had two other husbands Cleopas and Salome. From these three unions we are told that Anna had three daughters, all called Mary, and while one was the Mother of Christ, the others were called Mary Cleopas, and Mary the wife of Zebedee.

A curious legend is related to account for a custom, still prevalent in Persia, of calling all dyeing establishments " Christ Shops." It seems that when Our Lord was only a boy, He once ran into the shop of Salem, the dyer. There He saw a heap of garments to be dyed and flung them all into a vat full of Indian blue. When the dyer returned after a momentary absence, and saw what mischief the Christ Child had done, he wrung his hands in despair, for the garments had been sent to him that he might dye them in various colours according to the owners' taste. Jesus, seeing the dyer's sorrow, bade him dry his tears, and added: " Of whatever cloth thou wishest the colour changed, I will change it for thee." Then, while Salem stood there beside Him, He drew the garments out of the blue dye, but they came out of whatever colour the dyer wished, and all " who saw this miracle and prodigy praised God."

The boyhood of Christ closes with the eventful journey to Jerusalem which is recorded in the Scriptures. The legends add but few details to this scene, and only state that the Christ Child astonished all the rabbis by His great learning, not only in the law and prophecies, but in all the sciences, He expounding to them " the number of the spheres and celestial bodies, and their natures and operations, their opposition, trine, quartile, and sextile aspect, their direct course and retrogression, degrees and the sixtieths of degrees, and other things which reason does not attain unto."

After He had been found in the temple by Joseph and Mary, the gospels tell us that Christ returned to Nazareth, and was " subject " unto his parents, and that He " increased in wisdom and stature, and in favour with God and man." Some legends add that after twelve He became a Rabbi, and taught openly in the synagogue, but others aver that He lived a quiet and retired life, labouring hard at His work as a carpenter. In proof of this assertion the early Christians showed carefully-preserved ox-yokes, and rude utensils which they claimed had been made by Our Lord.

CHRIST DISPUTING WITH THE DOCTORS. (HOFMANN.)

CHAPTER VII.

THE MINISTRY OF CHRIST.

> History of Joseph the Carpenter — Joseph warned of death — Joseph's request — Mary's plea to Christ — The angels receive Joseph's soul — Joseph shrouded — The burial of Joseph — Christ's promise — Christ the carpenter — The Shadow of the Cross — The Baptism — The Temptation — The wedding at Cana — The wine measure — The goose — The woodpecker — The Virgin's terror — Story of Abgar — Description of Christ — The parting of Christ and His Mother — The Passion Play — The birth of Judas — Crimes and repentance of Judas — The treachery of Judas — The death of Judas — Judas in hell — The colour of Judas — The seamen and Judas — Leonardo da Vinci's Judas.

IT was probably some time during the early manhood of Christ that Joseph died. The Scriptures make no mention of this event, but we have a detailed account of it in a curious work entitled " History of Joseph the Carpenter." This is supposed to contain the account given by Our Lord himself, after the resurrection, while He sat on the Mount of Olives, instructing His chosen disciples.

This document is of such great antiquity that it is believed to have existed already in the second century of our era. It relates the first marriage of Joseph at forty, his conjugal life during forty-nine years, his short period of mourning, and his second marriage to Mary, whom he sheltered two whole years, before he was called upon to be the protector of the Infant Saviour.

By a miraculous dispensation of Providence, Joseph the Carpenter "laboured under no infirmity of body, his sight failed not, and no tooth in his mouth decayed, nor was he ever insane in mind in all his life; but, like a youth, he always displayed juvenile vigour in his affairs, and his members remained whole and free from all pain."

When he attained the advanced age of one hundred and eleven years, and his life had "been prolonged to the utmost limit," the archangel Michael made known to him that the hour of death was drawing near. Troubled by this announcement, Joseph went down to Jerusalem, and having gone into the temple, he fervently prayed that God would send down the archangel Michael, to attend upon his soul and body until they parted company. He also asked that his guardian angel might not forsake him, until he had been brought safely before the Judgment throne.

When Joseph reached home again, the shadow of death began to hover over him, and he became very ill. Mary, seeing his suffering, and perceiving that he was about to die, now begged her Son to save him. But Jesus, looking down upon her with infinite compassion, gently answered: "O my mother, most loving, surely upon all creatures which are born in this world, lieth the same necessity of dying; for death hath dominion over all the human race. Thou also, O my virgin mother, must expect the same end of life with all other mortals. Nevertheless, thy death, as also the death of this pious man, is not death, but perennial life forever. But it behoveth me too to die, as respects the body which I received from thee. But arise, O my venerable mother, go and enter to Joseph, the blessed old man, that thou mayest see what happeneth when his soul goes up from his body."

Thus adjured Mary went back to her place at Joseph's bedside, where she sat holding his hand, and anxiously awaiting the end. Christ, too, shared this painful watch, and placing His hand upon Joseph's breast He finally " perceived his soul already near his throat preparing to depart from its receptacle." This strange statement is made on the strength of an ancient belief which was still current several centuries after the beginning of our era, that the soul, clad in the material form of a tiny new-born infant, a bird, or even a mouse, escaped through the mouth at the moment of death.

After Joseph had taken an affectionate farewell of all his family, he bewailed his sinfulness and cursed every part of his body, from his eyes, " which have looked upon offence," to his feet, " which have too often walked in ways displeasing to God." His children, Mary, and Jesus, who were all standing around him, wept aloud and lamented.

Christ alone was not so overcome by His sorrow, that He could not notice what was happening, and looking up suddenly He saw " Death now coming, and all Gehenna with it, crowded with its hosts and attendants; and their garments, faces, and mouths cast out fire." Joseph too perceived the infernal legions, and groaned so loud that Christ earnestly prayed His Father to send down the angels Michael and Gabriel, with all the heavenly host, to drive away the demons and take possession of the good man's soul.

In answer to this appeal the angels came, wrapped Joseph's soul in a garment of dazzling purity, and carried it off to heaven. By Christ's command some of the angels also wrapped his body in a miraculous winding-sheet, so that it should never see corruption. The chief men of the place, coming a few moments later to perform this pious duty, were unable to unfasten this shroud, which adhered to the body like iron, and in which they could find no edges.

The friends now bore Joseph to his last resting-place in the sepulchre of his fathers. When they returned home, Jesus, remembering all the good man had done for Him in His helpless infancy, promised that his body should be preserved entire until the millennium, pronounced his eulogy, and added the following words: " And whatever mortal is mindful of the oblation on the day of thy memorial, him will I bless and reward in the congregation of virgins. And whoever giveth to the wretched, and poor, and widows, and orphans, of the work of his hands on the day when thy memory is celebrated, and in thy name, he shall not be without good all the days of his life. Whoever, also, shall offer to drink a cup of water or of wine to the widow or orphan in thy name, I will give him to thee, that thou mayest go in with him to the banquet of a thousand years. And every man that shall attend to the oblation on the day of thy commemoration, I will bless him, and give him a recompense in the church of virgins; I will return him (I say) thirty, sixty, and one hundred for one. And whosoever writeth the history of thy life, thy labour, and thy departure from this world, and this discourse delivered by my mouth, I will commit him to thy guardianship while he shall remain in this life. And when his soul departeth from his body, and when he must leave this world, I will burn the book of his sins, nor will I torment him with any punishment in the day of judgment; but he shall cross the fiery sea, and shall traverse it without difficulty and pain. This is incumbent upon every needy man who cannot do any of the things which I have mentioned,—that if a son is born to him, he shall call his name Joseph. So neither poverty nor sudden death shall have place in that house forever."

Needless to state that the above account of the death of Joseph, from which we have quoted freely to give an idea of the quaintness of the work in which it is recorded, has never been believed by any religious sect. The Roman Catholics honour Joseph as a saint, and keep the anniversary of his death on the 19th of March, but they only venture to conjecture that Joseph died a holy and peaceful death, cared for to the very end by his Virgin spouse and adopted Son.

> "Thrice happy saint of God, whose dying breath
> Was poured forth in the fond encircling arms
> Of Jesus and of Mary, glorious death,
> That knew no fears, no terrors, or alarms."
>
> D. FRENCH, *Tr.*: *Hymn to St. Joseph.*

Tradition relates that from the time of Joseph's death until the beginning of His public career, Christ, now the sole breadwinner of the little family, laboured hard at His trade as a carpenter. This natural conclusion, which has sanctified manual work in our eyes, has encouraged artists to represent Our Lord in the humble carpenter shop at Bethlehem. In one of these pictures, Mary, gazing at the gifts of the Magi, the crown, sceptre, and censer of gold, and musing upon the many strange things which had occurred and which all seemed to point toward an unusual destiny for her only Son, suddenly raises her head to look at Him. It is just the hour of evening prayer, and the weary Saviour, with hands and eyes upraised, is holding silent communion with His heavenly Father.

Mary looks upon Him with reverent awe for a moment, and then cowers down terrified, for the setting sun has cast His shadow against the wall, where the joists and tools help to form a ghastly representation of the coming Crucifixion. The shadow of the crown of gold assumes the appearance of the spiked crown of thorns, while the sceptre looks like the fatal lance, and the censer like the vessel in which the guards gave Him vinegar to drink.

> " One eve, they say,
> The shadow of His outstretched arms, cast strong
> By sun-down's low-shot light, painted a cross
> Black on the wall; and Mary, trembling, drew
> Her garment o'er the lattice. But He spake:
> "Near unto me is near to loss and death,
> And far from me is far from Life and gain."
>
> Sir EDWIN ARNOLD: *The Light of the World.*[1]

The legends are strangely silent concerning these years of preparation; even the beginning of His ministry and the Baptism in the Jordan are left in nearly all their Scriptural brevity and dignity. The only legendary additions to the account of the Baptism are that the angels were present and held His garments, and that as He came up out of the waters they were changed into a mass of glowing fire.

The scene of the temptation was, however, so congenial to the minds of early writers,

---

[1] Funk and Wagnall.

SHADOW OF DEATH. (Holman Hunt.)

that they have greatly enlarged upon it, and have depicted Christ subject to as many and peculiar temptations as St. Anthony during his sojourn in the desert. The ministering of the angels at the end of the forty days' fast, is also related with all the realistic simplicity of the Middle Ages, and there are several old pictures which represent Christ as being led to a board sumptuously spread with all manner of tempting viands, and with such mediæval luxuries as peacocks served up in all the glory of their brilliant plumage. This scene, introducing the devil whose tricks always pleased the public, was one of the favourite parts in the old miracle play, of which we give a fragment here in all its quaintness of language and orthography:—

"Lo, how saye ye now? is not here a pleasant sight?
If ye wyll, ye maye here have all the world's delyght.
Here is to be seane the kyngedom of Arabye,
With all the regyons of Affryck, Europe and Asye,
And their whole delightes, their pompe, their magnifycence.
Their ryches, their honour, their welth, their concupyscence,
Here is golde and sylver in wonderfull habundaunce,
Sylkes, velvetes, tyssues, with wynes and spyces of plesaunce:
Here are fayre women, of countenance ameable,
With all kyndes of meales to the body dylectable:

> Here are camels, stoute horses, and mules that never
>   wyll tyre,
> With so many pleasures as your heart can desyre."
>
> JOHAN BALE: *Christ's Temptation.*

The Scriptures mention the fact that Mary was present at the wedding at Cana, and tradition adds that the bride and groom were John the Evangelist and Mary Magdalene, who immediately after the feast devoted themselves entirely to the service of Christ, leading the austere lives of a monk and nun.

Some Roman Catholics aver that the time for the public manifestation of Christ's power had not yet come, but that constrained, as it were, by His mother's wishes He was forced to anticipate it. "Thus it was that the Blessed Virgin had the first fruits of the miracles of her divine Son, and that her intercession caused even the will of God to bend in her favour." Because Mary's prayers thus prevailed upon this one occasion, her worshippers still credit them with equal power at all times, and hence consider her as a powerful mediator.

As Christ sometimes passed out of Galilee, and once even visited Perea and the land thereabout, where He preached the Gospel to the Gentiles, mediæval writers have liked to imagine that He wandered still further afield, and even visited the principal parts of Europe. Hence there are extant a number of traditions, connecting His name with some noted place or subject.

Among these peculiar fancies we have, for instance, a Moselle legend, where we are told that Christ once wandered along the banks of this picturesque stream, accompanied by His small but devoted band of disciples. It was in summer, the heat was overpowering, and as they came within sight of the town of Coblentz, situated at the junction of the Rhine and Moselle, Christ sat down by the roadside, and bade Peter go to the city, and purchase a measure of wine so that they might all drink and be refreshed.

Provided with a small sum, taken from Judas' jealously guarded purse, Peter sped on to the inn, where he bought a wooden measure filled to the very brim with wine of the country's growth. Peter immediately set out on his return journey, but he had scarcely taken a few steps, when the wine overflowed, and a few drops of the refreshing draught fell down upon the dry sand of the road, where they were quickly absorbed.

The waste of such good wine seemed nothing less than wicked to Peter, and reasoning that it would be far better to drink the surplus than to lose it thus, he applied his parched lips to the rim of the vessel. His thirst was so great that he drew a deeper draught than he intended, and when he raised his head he perceived, with dismay, that the measure no longer seemed full. In his anxiety to conceal his wrong-doing, and afraid lest the Master should comment upon the space between the wine and the top of the vessel, Peter now had recourse to his knife, and carefully pared down the measure until it again seemed quite full. Then he resumed his journey. After a few steps, however, the wine again overflowed; the same reasoning took place, and Peter's thirsty lips made such a difference in the contents of the vessel, that he was again forced to resort to his knife.

Thus sipping and snipping, Peter continued his way, and by the time he reached his companions, the measure was reduced to such small dimensions, that only a tiny draught of wine remained in the now shallow vessel. The Saviour gazed at it for a moment in silence, and then calmly remarked, "What miserably small measures the people here sell!" Then He added that as there was barely enough wine in the vessel to moisten the lips of a single person, Peter might keep it as his share, for he liked the taste of the native vintage, as the drops of wine still clinging to his beard plainly testified.

While the crestfallen Peter withdrew to one side, to drink the wine allotted to him, the Redeemer called the disciples around Him, and by a miracle provided generously for all their wants. Ever since this occurrence the people along the banks of the Moselle have used shallow measures for their wine, and these vessels have always been called, "Miseräbelchen," or miserable little things, in memory of the contemptuous epithet applied to them by Our Lord.[1]

Another legend relates that Christ and his disciples, in the course of one of the excursions in Germany, once came to an inn, where there was no food to be had except a lonely goose still waddling near the door. The innkeeper offered to serve this fowl for their breakfast upon the morrow, and when one of the disciples discontentedly muttered that the bird would scarcely be enough for a single guest, Our Lord exclaimed: "Very well, the goose shall be the portion of the one among you who dreams the best dream."

The weary disciples now retired, and anxious to woo the desired dream they were soon sound asleep. All slept heavily, except Judas, who,

[1] See the author's Legends of the Rhine. A. S. Barnes & Co.

after thinking over the few chances in his favour, fancied that it would be better to make sure of the goose by killing and eating it overnight. Without waking his companions, he softly went in search of the fowl, which he deftly killed, plucked, and cooked, and when he had eaten it he went back to bed.

Early the next morning Judas was awakened by the clatter of the disciples' tongues, for they were all eagerly relating their dreams, and each loudly claimed that his was the best. After listening to their dispute for some time in silence, Judas said, "Hold, friends, my dream was the best of all, for methought I ate the goose."

The disciples were not ready to acknowledge his claim, and went in search of the disputed fowl. Of course they could not find it, and when they finally discovered its feathers and bones, Judas calmly remarked: "I told you my dream was the best, and I am now inclined to think that it was a reality."

Another very peculiar legend is told in Norway, in connection with the red-crested black woodpecker. It is as follows: Once when Our Lord and St. Peter were wandering together upon earth, they came to the house of a woman who was busy baking her bread. This woman was named Gertrude; she was remarkably quick in all her movements, and flitted hither and thither in her kitchen, in her trim dress and with a bright-red hood upon her head.

Looking in at the open door, Christ begged this woman to bake a little loaf for Him, because He and His companion had tasted no food since early morning and were nearly famished. Gertrude glanced at the Saviour, and then taking a very small pinch of dough, she deftly moulded it into a tiny loaf, which she set on the fire to bake. To her surprise it swelled out and grew so large that it soon filled the whole pan.

The woman thought such a loaf far too large for alms, so she set it aside, and taking a smaller piece of dough, baked a second loaf, which turned out even larger than the first. This too was reserved for her own family, while she made a third attempt to bake a very small loaf. When that failed also, the grasping woman said to the Saviour: "You must go without alms, for all my bakings are too large for you."

This niggardliness so incensed Our Lord, that He turned upon the woman and said: "Because thou gavest me nothing, thou shalt for a punishment become a little bird, shalt seek thy dry food between the wood and the bark, and drink only when it rains."

Hardly were these words spoken when the

woman was transformed into a woodpecker (known in Norway as the Gertrud Bird). She flew away through the kitchen chimney, where the soot made her dress very black, but did not dim the bright scarlet of her hood. Since then, the woodpecker constantly taps the bark of the trees with its strong bill, to secure its sustenance, and its harsh cry or whistle is a call for rain, so that it can quench the thirst which cannot else be satisfied.

The authentic narrative of Our Lord's sayings and doings is too well known to require any mention here, and the legends have ventured to add but little to the Bible account. Some commentators are of the opinion that the Virgin Mary, with a few other devoted women, followed Him throughout His ministry, but others suppose that she remained at home, where her Son visited her from time to time.

She was, we are told, warned of Christ's peril when the angry people of Nazareth led Him to the brow of the hill upon which their city was built, with the avowed intention of casting Him down headlong. Trembling with fear, Mary ran thither as fast as she could, but, overcome by her emotions, she sank fainting upon a spot which is still dedicated to "Our Lady del Tremore."

The fame of Christ's miracles had in the

mean time spread far and wide, and had even come to the ears of Abgar, or Abgarus, king of Macedonia. This monarch, suffering keenly from an incurable disease, now penned a letter to Christ, imploring Him to come to his aid, and offering to share his throne with Him. This epistle, which is preserved in the apocrypha, and which Eusebius and some modern writers consider genuine, was entrusted to the care of Ananias, a painter. The messenger hastened to Palestine, delivered the letter, and Christ, touched by Abgar's evident faith, wrote an answer, promising to send one of His disciples to Edessa after His ascension.

Ananias, hoping to give his master some idea of the beauty of Christ's countenance, once tried to sketch His portrait while He was exhorting the multitude as usual. The Redeemer, noticing the painter's vain efforts, and perceiving that he was dazzled by the radiance of His countenance, now called Ananias to Him. Then, taking either the canvas upon which the painter had fruitlessly striven to paint His features, or a cloth, He wiped His face upon it. The painter, receiving this cloth from the hands of the Redeemer, was surprised to see that it bore a perfect imprint of His divine countenance.

The legend goes on to relate that Ananias departed with this relic; but, becoming afraid of it for some mysterious reason, he buried it under a heap of rubbish lying by the road-side. People passing by became aware of a strange yet steady light which shone forth from the rubbish, and upon seeking to ascertain what produced it, they found the cloth. The bricks lying near it were now seen to bear the same imprint of Our Lord's face. Some writers claim that the cloth given by Christ to Ananias, and preserved at Rome or Genoa, cured Abgar as soon as he gazed upon it; but others assert that the king was healed only when Thaddeus came to him, as Christ had promised. Abgar was not only cured, but he became an enthusiastic convert, and his city was one of the strongholds of the new faith. Christ's letter to Abgar, which is also preserved in the apocrypha, is undoubtedly a forgery, although there is some cause to think that Abgar may have been the author of the epistle ascribed to him.

The oldest description now extant of Christ's physical appearance is that contained in the apocrypha, and purporting to have been written by Lentulus, a contemporary of the Redeemer, and an eye-witness of some of His miracles.

The description is interesting, if not authentic, and runs thus: "There has appeared in our times a man of tall stature, beautiful, with a venerable countenance, which they who look on it can both love and fear. His hair is waving and crisp, somewhat wine-coloured, and glittering as it flows down over His shoulders, with a parting in the middle, after the manner of the Nazarenes. His brow is smooth and most serene; His face is without any spot or wrinkle, and glows with a delicate flush. His nose and mouth are of faultless contour; the beard is abundant and hazel-coloured like His hair, not long but forked. His eyes are prominent, brilliant, and change their colour. In denunciation, He is terrible, calm and loving in admonition, cheerful but with unimpaired dignity. He has never been seen to laugh, but oftentimes to weep. His hands and limbs are beautiful to look upon. In speech He is grave, reserved, modest, and He is fair among the children of men."

Strangely at variance with this description, to which artists have more or less conformed, is the belief, current at one time among Christians, that Jesus was ill-favoured, deformed, and utterly wanting in all outward graces or attractions. Fortunately for art, this fashion soon died out, and artists have since striven to represent the beauty of the bodily temple of the One who was "all glorious within."

It is supposed that before starting out upon His last eventful journey to celebrate the Passover at Jerusalem, Christ took an affectionate leave of His Virgin mother. She was very sad, for she felt that the time was near, when the sword prophesied by the aged Simeon would pierce her breast. The parting scene, often represented in art, was also incorporated in the Mysteries, or religious plays, which were current until the time of Shakespeare, and which, in a very modified form, still subsist in the Passion Play given at Oberammergau every ten years. This dramatic presentation of the Life and Suffering of Our Lord, is given by the peasants of the community, with the deepest feelings of reverence, in consequence of a vow made in 1634, at the time when an awful plague was causing great ravages in the village and neighbourhood. The vow has been faithfully kept, and every ten years the Passion Play has been given there, in an open-air theatre constructed for that express purpose.

With the increased facilities for travel, throngs

CHRIST TAKES LEAVE OF HIS MOTHER. (PLOCKHORST.)

of people from all countries have hastened thither for all the representations, and we have descriptions of the play and of the impression which it produces upon the spectators, from the pens of several able writers. The scene of the final parting between Mother and Son is, it seems, particularly affecting, and while it is taking place the chorus sings : —

> "Ah, they come, the parting hours!
> Deepest wounds they now inflict,
> Mary, on thy heart!
> Ah, thy Son must leave thee now
> On the cross to faint, to die; —
> Who can weigh the mother's woe?"
>
> *Passion Play at Oberammergau.*

Many legends are connected with the closing scenes of Our Lord's career upon earth. They have served as themes for poets and painters, and are hence worthy of notice, although they jar upon modern taste. The creations of the fertile brains of long successions of pilgrims, preachers, and minstrels, who were debarred from access to the Scriptures by the rarity of manuscript copies, — these tales, which at first seem very irreverent, were the natural outcome of the prevalent ignorance.

As the Last Supper is one of the most important events of Our Lord's life at this epoch, and came so soon after the parting at Nazareth, and the triumphant entrance into Jerusalem, many traditions have naturally been connected with it.

The personality, for instance, of one of the guests, Judas, is brought forcibly to our notice. Except in direct connection with his heinous crime, Judas is seldom mentioned in the Scriptures; but where the inspired writers remained silent, the legends delight in furnishing many a grewsome detail. Judas' betrayal of the Lord deservedly made him a by-word, and poets and painters have constantly vied with one another in depicting him in the most repulsive colours.

As nothing seemed too bad to say or write of this traitor, the minstrels and playwrights of the Middle Ages gave their imagination free play, and combining all the most horrible incidents found in the classical literature of the heathen world, they gradually evolved the following legend, or series of legends, about him.

Judas, the traitor, belonged by birth to the tribe of Reuben, and even before he came into the world his mother dreamt that her child would be accursed. Like Œdipus, he was to murder his father and marry his mother; but instead of causing the downfall of his native country, like his prototype, Judas was destined to sell his God.

Terrified by this awful dream, the woman hastened to impart it to her husband, and together they decided that it would be wiser that the child should perish, than live to finish such an unenviable career. When the child was born they had not the courage to kill him themselves, but entrusted him to a servant who exposed him in a cask or chest, like Perseus, to the fury of the waves. The sea, however, refused to keep Judas, and cast him ashore, where he was found and adopted by a benevolent king and queen.

Evil by nature, Judas repaid their care with base ingratitude, quarrelled with his playmates, and after a disagreeable childhood slew the king's own son. Soon after this he killed the monarch himself on account of a dispute over a game of chess. This bloody result of a peaceful game is, by the way, a favourite incident in mediæval literature, and appears in nearly all the noted romances of the period.

Afraid of punishment for these crimes, Judas now fled, and after some wandering, reached Judea, where he became a page of Pontius Pilate. While in the latter's service, driven on by relentless fate, Judas fell into a brawl with his own father, whom he slew, and sometime after, he married his unfortunate mother. She discovered his identity only too late, and in despair revealed to him the secret of his birth.

In spite of his innate wickedness, Judas was so horror-struck at this revelation, that hearing of Christ's power to forgive sins, he eagerly went in search of Him, and falling at His feet implored His aid. Although cognizant of all things, and well aware of the fact that Judas would eventually betray Him, Our Lord received the sinner among His chosen band of followers, and made him keeper of the common purse.

Judas had already been the victim of every vice, except avarice. He now became a prey to this failing also, which he carried to the utmost extreme, secretly begrudging every penny which he was obliged to expend, and openly bewailing the waste of the precious ointment which Mary Magdalene poured out upon the feet of Our Lord. It was by an appeal to his last besetting sin, avarice, that the Sanhedrim, after much chaffering, induced him to deliver up Christ into their power for thirty pieces of silver.

The narrative now follows the Scriptures closely, merely adding that Judas designated Jesus by a kiss, because there was such a strong resemblance between Him and James the

Less, that the guards might else have arrested the wrong man. The treason accomplished, Judas, struck with sudden horror, flung the thirty pieces of silver on the temple floor, and rushing out wildly, filled the measure of his awful iniquities by committing suicide.

> "He now runs raving to and fro,
> And finds no rest for evermore.
> Till he, alas! torn by despair,
> Casts from him in bewilder'd haste
> The intol'rable load of life."
> *Passion Play at Oberammergau.*

Tradition relates that Judas hung himself either upon an elder-tree, which Sir John Mandeville, the fourteenth century traveller, claims to have seen, or upon an aspen, whose trembling is ascribed to the horror felt by the tree at bearing such fruit.

> "On the morrow stood she trembling,
> At the awful weight she bore,
> When the sun in midnight blackness
> Darkened on Judæa's shore.
> Still, when not a breeze is stirring,
> When the mist sleeps on the hill,
> And all other trees are moveless,
> Stands the aspen trembling still."

In some of the mediæval Passion Plays, which were so popular during more than six centuries,

Judas repents when he sees Christ before the Judgment seat of Pilate. He rushes madly away, and Remorse, a real actor, taking possession of him, torments him so unmercifully that, unable to endure further torture, he calls for Despair, also a real person.

Thus summoned, Despair grimly advises him to commit suicide, and glibly enumerates all the various modes by which he can do so. He even, in his anxiety to help Judas, proffers the necessary implements, with all the persuasive airs and speeches of a chapman setting forth his wares to tempt a reluctant buyer. Judas, after much wavering, finally selects a rope and goes forth to hang himself.

To represent everything as realistically as possible, some of these mediæval Mysteries were played upon stages divided into three horizontal parts. The upper part was reserved for God, Christ, the Virgin Mary, and the angels. The middle was supposed to be the earth, where the principal part of the play was performed, and the lowest stage was reserved for the demons. The mouth of hell was shown either as the gaping jaws of a huge monster, as an immense kettle, or as a bottomless pit, whence rose smoke and blue flames.

The dénouement of the Judas story, which

is given in the Scriptures with graphic brevity, "he burst asunder in the midst, and all his bowels gushed out," was carried out in these plays with the utmost fidelity, to gratify the public taste for horrors. The demons in the lower space then came out, and greedily snatched and gobbled up the sausages provided to simulate Judas's intestines, when the catastrophe occurred. But even this realistic performance was not enough to satisfy the mediæval imagination, for we are also told that Judas's soul, unable to escape through the lips which had given that fatal kiss, left his body with the bowels. The Devil or his emissaries then pounced upon it, and dragged it down to hell, where Satan, rising from his throne to do homage to one whose wickedness surpassed his own, welcomed Judas with a kiss!

Another account relates that Judas was too sinful even for hell, and that his soul was tossed like a ball from one demon to another, none of them wishing to undertake the endless task of punishing such a superlative sinner. This superstition has been used by some of the early masters, who also represent Judas's suicide and entrance into the Lower Regions.

The instruction, and shall we say the amusement, given to the people by the Mysteries was considered of such advantage and importance, that, even at the time of the Reformation, and after the invention of printing, Luther warmly advocated them, saying they were far more effective than many sermons in bringing out the moral teachings of the Holy Writ. The very first of these plays was composed, as far as we know, in the fourth century, and was attributed to Gregory Nazianzen. Given at first only on the great church days, by the clergy, in the church itself, the throng of spectators soon became so great that the play had to be performed in the church porch or in the graveyard. But the desecration of the graves by the tramp of many feet could not long be endured, so the stage was set up in the market-place, or on a large meadow outside of the city. Then the plays ceased to be given by the priests and monks themselves, and were represented by chartered companies of strolling actors, or by the various guilds of the large towns.

The Mysteries continued to win applause until the eighteenth century, when they were forbidden by law. They had by this time outlived their usefulness, and had so degenerated, that instead of being, as they were first intended, a means of edification, they had become, on the contrary, a stumbling block to many.

Thanks to the vivid representation they gave of the infamous career of the traitor Judas, he was generally abhorred. As he appeared on the stage, in a garment of dirty yellow, this colour was soon considered as the badge of infamy, and none but criminals ever wore it. Even now, the galley slaves in Spain and Italy still wear a garb of that hue; and we are told that the Jews in Venice were compelled by law to wear yellow hats all through the Middle Ages, as an outward mark of the estimation in which they were then held by all Christians.

In most paintings Judas is represented as very repulsive-looking, but tradition says he bore a close resemblance to Our Lord. The Mohammedans add, that, owing to this similarity of feature, "God devised a stratagem" against the Jews, and caused them to crucify Judas instead of Jesus, who was snatched up into heaven bodily by the angel Gabriel, and was not allowed to taste of death.

We are told that Portuguese and South American sailors still observe a yearly ceremony called the flogging of Judas Iscariot. A block of wood, rudely carved to imitate the betrayer, is clad in a sailor's suit and publicly hanged early in the morning. At about eleven A. M. this figure is lowered into the water, and ducked three times. Then it is again hoisted on board the vessel, and after it has been kicked about to the sailors' content, it is lashed to the mast, where all hands flog it with knotted ropes until its garments have been cut to pieces. The ship's bell, in the mean while, keeps up a constant tolling, and all the men who are not engaged in flogging the effigy, chant denunciations against it, until this peculiar ceremony is ended by the burning of the dummy which represents the arch-traitor.

In pictures representing the beginning of the Last Supper, the figure of Judas is never omitted. We are informed that while Leonardo da Vinci was at work on his masterpiece, which has, alas! nearly entirely fallen into decay, he searched long and vainly for a model for Judas. The prior of the convent, a rude and ignorant man, once ventured to chide the painter for progressing so slowly. Leonardo da Vinci tried to excuse himself by explaining his difficulty; but the prior, knowing nothing of a painter's requirements, impatiently exclaimed that any man would do. These words so nettled the artist that he gravely promised to finish the picture in a few days provided the prior were willing to sit for Judas! Of course the prior did not accept the invitation, but he was so taken aback by the mere proposal that he never ventured to hurry the artist again.

The common superstition, concerning the unluckiness of the number thirteen, is also connected with the celebration of the Last Supper. And, because one of the thirteen who sat down to the board died upon the Cross shortly after, people have since said that whenever thirteen guests sit down to the same table, one of them is sure to be called away within the year.

CHAPTER VIII.

THE PASSION WEEK.

The Last Supper — Lucifer's crown — Revolt of Lucifer — Man's downfall planned — The legend of Israfil — Banishment of Adam and Eve — The Holy Grail — The blood of Christ — Joseph in prison — Vespasian and Getus — Veronica's handkerchief — The first crusade — The Holy Grail in France — The Round Table — The Siege Perilous — The Holy Grail in England — Christ before Pilate — The officer — The standards — Procla's dream — The witnesses — The sentence.

ONE of the most important mediæval legends, that of the Holy Grail, is intimately connected with the Last Supper, to which as a rule, tradition has ventured to make very few additions. The above mentioned legend relates either to the dish in which Our Lord dipped the sop which He handed to Judas, or to the cup in which He gave His disciples the sacramental wine.

Tradition relates that, long before the creation of Adam and Eve, God once forsook his throne

SAINT MICHAEL.

to view the earth, his new creation, and pronounce it good. Lucifer, one of the highest among his angels, seeing the heavenly throne temporarily vacant, ventured to seat himself upon it, and to claim the worship of the angels, some of whom did homage to him. To show their reverence for Lucifer, these subservient creatures further tendered him a marvelous crown, studded with countless stones of great price, which they set upon his head, calling him their king. Such insolence on the part of the angel and his adherents was, however, soon to be punished; for, although the rebels banded their forces together, they could not resist the onslaught of the celestial host, led by Michael, and the War in Heaven ended with the downfall of the insurgents.

Lucifer and all his crew were then hurled headlong out of heaven, and in the fall one of the precious stones, detached from the crown, dropped down upon the earth unnoticed. Michael and his angels closely pursued the demon crew, who, losing their angelic form and attributes as they fell, were finally pinioned fast in the Infernal Regions, which were henceforth to be their abode. This legend, so magnificently embodied by Milton in our greatest English epic, Paradise Lost, has also been the theme of

Caedmon, and was embodied in the religious plays of the Middle Ages.

The next stage in the narrative sets forth Lucifer's plan to seduce the newly created human pair and make them disobey their Creator. To prevent any harm from happening to Adam and Eve, a more recent legend tells us that God bade his angels keep close watch around the garden of Eden as long as the nightly shadows made it possible for any one to enter Paradise unseen. The guard was faithfully kept, until Israfil, one of the younger angels, prompted by curiosity, forsook his post and went to gaze upon the sleeping Eve. During his temporary absence, Satan entered the Garden unperceived, and, on the very next day, induced Eve to eat of the forbidden fruit, and forfeit the life of endless bliss promised her.

The legend then goes on to relate that the curse did not fall only upon the serpent, Adam, and Eve, but that God also punished Israfil, whom he condemned to be the angel of destruction and death.

> "When in the evening cool the Lord appears,
> Sees the forbidden tree with broken bloom,
> The garden desolate and lost in gloom,
> The mortals hiding from his searching gaze,
> Israfil, speechless, hears

Their fate pronounced, sees their repentant tears,
And death's dread shadow hanging o'er their days.
And now on him the rays
Of the Eternal Vision fall, the word
Of his own doom is heard:
'Since death by thee is come unto the earth,
Be thou its messenger. Thy name shall be
A terror unto all of human birth:
The shadow of the grave forever follow thee.'"

      Mrs. FRANCES L. MACE: *Israfil*.[1]

The angel, who had never seen death and knew not what it meant, cowered with apprehension. He wandered out into the Garden after the Lord had gone, and gently handled the flowers, which, to his horror, were blighted by his touch. Now he knew the meaning of the curse which had been pronounced upon him, and realized that he would be called upon to rob all animate things of their dearest possession, — life!

"In a bitter grief
He murmured, 'This is death!
And this henceforth shall be my destiny:
To slay, but not to die, —
To blight all things of mortal breath;
All earthly loveliness to sear;
All that you beings hold most dear
Must perish when my steps draw near.
Nor can I shun my fearful power,

[1] Harper's Magazine, May, 1877.

> Or spare them from one dreaded hour.
> Onward I go through all the years,
> Unheeding human prayers and tears.
> Let mortals seek through toil and fears
> Some transient gleams of love and joy,—
> I follow after to destroy.'"
>
> Mrs. FRANCES L. MACE: *Israfil*.[1]

Israfil could not have endured this prospect, had not the Son of God suddenly appeared to him then, and revealed that God had given the Redeemer the power of restoring life to the dead flowers and birds, and that He would also give everlasting life and happiness to all those whom Israfil had slain.

> "Then spake He: 'Israfil,
> The Father to the Son a boon hath given.
> Go forth, but I am with thee. Do his will
> Who laid this doom upon thee, and be still.
> Thou dost destroy, but thus can I restore.
> Angel of death, arise, and hope once more!
> From Abel's blood spilt on the altar stone,
> To Calvary's cross which I must bear alone,
> Thou shalt be terrible to human kind,
> And hope but dimly light the troubled mind;
> But from that grave which yields to me its portal,
> Faith shall come forth, the comforter immortal,
> And thou, new crowned, shalt be
> Seen by believing eyes linked hand in hand with me.'"
>
> Mrs. FRANCES L. MACE: *Israfil*.[1]

[1] Harper's Magazine, May, 1877.

Thus comforted, the sad-faced angel of death went forth to do God's will, and carried destruction wherever he passed. He visited first Abel, then Adam and the lovely Eve, whom he had so much admired, and dogged the footsteps of all the human race.

It was one of the direct descendants of Adam and Eve who found the precious stone which had fallen from Lucifer's crown, and fashioned from it a priceless cup. After many centuries, this vessel came into the hands of Joseph of Arimathea, in whose house Christ kept the feast of the Passover with his disciples. When the Crucifixion followed so closely upon the Last Supper, Joseph took this cup, and standing beneath the Cross, received into it a few drops of the blood of Our Lord. It was owing to this circumstance that the vessel was called Sangraal, Sangreal, or Holy Grail, for the divine blood had not only sanctified it, but had given it miraculous powers which soon became manifest.

The Jews, afraid lest Caesar should claim the body of Christ, — which they could not produce, — resolved to kill Joseph of Arimathea immediately after the Resurrection, and then to accuse him of having stolen and concealed the body of our Lord. To keep this murder a secret, Joseph was taken by night, and placed in a sealed prison-cell, where the Jews fancied he would soon die. But here he was marvelously fed and sustained by the Holy Grail, which filled his prison with beams of refulgent, life-giving light.

The mediæval legend, regardless of such trifling matters as history, chronology, or even probability, now goes on to relate that a knight, returning from Palestine, related the Passion of Our Lord to the Emperor Vespasian. The latter's curiosity was so aroused, that he sent a commission into Judea to investigate the matter, and especially to bring back some holy relic, which might relieve him of a painful disease. This, the early writers gravely assert, was a wasp's nest in his nose, and he hoped the relic would also cure his son Titus of leprosy.

On their return, the ambassadors gave Pilate's account of the trial and Crucifixion. Then, when Vespasian clamoured for a relic, they presented to him a woman called Berenice, or Veronica, who had been cured of an issue of blood by touching the garments of Our Lord, as He once passed through a crowded street.

In her gratitude for her miraculous cure Veronica loved the Saviour and longed for a portrait of Him. According to one version of the story, Saint Luke painted her a picture, which was quite satisfactory until she compared it with the model. But another version relates that Christ met her as she was carrying the canvas to St. Luke, took it from her hand, and burying His face in it for a moment, handed it back to her stamped with His divine features. A third version claims that Christ, aware of Veronica's desire to obtain a portrait, once went to her house to supper, and that, asking for water and a towel, He washed His face and left His imprint upon the cloth He used to wipe it dry.

The fourth version of the story, is, however, the one generally adopted by poets and painters. In it we are told that on the way to Calvary, Christ fell beneath His cross, which He was forced to carry to the place of torture. The faithful women, who had followed Him all through His ministry, did not desert Him now, but knelt by the roadside, weeping bitterly. As He fell, He saw their mournful faces, and tenderly addressing them said: "Women of Jerusalem, weep not for me."

The perspiration on His brow, and the blood which flowed from the cruel wounds inflicted by the crown of thorns, seemed for a moment to obstruct His sight, so Veronica offered Him her veil, with which He wiped His face ere He passed on. It was on this piece of linen, called the Sudarium, or Vera Icon, that His features were stamped, and Veronica piously kept it as her greatest treasure, although she also possessed a very life-like statue of Our Lord, which was placed in front of her house at Paneas.

No sooner had Vespasian and Titus gazed upon Veronica's portrait of Christ, which she had refused to entrust to any one's keeping, and had brought to Rome herself, than they were miraculously cured of their painful diseases. They naturally questioned Veronica closely about Jesus, and learning from her how cruelly the Jews had treated Him, Vespasian set out for Palestine at the head of a large army. Thus, in mediæval literature, the siege of Jerusalem by the Romans, is made to appear as a Holy War, and is called the First Crusade!

When Jerusalem had been taken, Vespasian and Titus vainly tried to make the Jews give up the body of Christ, which they wanted to secure as a most precious relic. But all the Jews insisted that Joseph had stolen it, and Vespasian put one of their number under torture to discover the truth.

This man remained silent as long as he could, but finally confessed that Joseph had been secretly walled up in a prison-cell about a year before. To ascertain the truth of this confession, Vespasian had the wall torn down, and he was surprised to see Joseph of Arimathea come out alive and well, and to hear him greet him by his imperial title and name. Although delivered from prison by miracle, Joseph of Arimathea feared further persecutions on the part of the Jews. So he left Jerusalem, went to Joppa, and there embarked on a waiting vessel with his sister and brother-in-law. They sailed away, and after a long journey landed at Marseilles, in France, still bearing with them the Holy Grail, which continued to provide for all their wants.

Besides supplying them with the food and drink they liked best, the Holy Grail, whose beneficent powers were renewed every Good Friday, — because a dove then came down from heaven bearing a consecrated wafer which was deposited in the cup, — cured them when they were ill, and served as an oracle. When Joseph and his friends did not know what to do, they spent a certain time in preparation and prayer before they uncovered the Holy Grail. Upon its luminous edge they could then read, in letters of flame, commands which none of them ever ventured to disobey.

Joseph of Arimathea, and his little band of faithful followers, were perfectly happy in

France, until one of their number committed a secret but grievous sin. Plague and famine broke out in the country, and Joseph, hoping to discover and punish the sinner, consulted the Holy Grail. By its orders he built a Round Table, and made a supper to which all were invited. Then, warned by the Holy Grail that the culprit would be designated by a miracle, Joseph watched each guest closely as he took his seat. When it came to the turn of Moses, the sinner, to take his place at the board, the ground opened, and swallowed him up, and the prediction was made that the seat which he had occupied should be called the "Siege Perilous," because it would be fatal to all sinners who ventured to sit in it.

Shortly after this event, Joseph of Arimathea was warned in a vision that the Siege Perilous would be worthily occupied by one of his own decendants, a stainless knight. Then, after sojourning for some time in France with the Holy Grail, Joseph carried it to Glastonbury, in England. Reaching this point, which tradition identifies with the spot where Alfred watched the cakes in the herdsman's hut, and with the fabled land of Avalon, " where falls not hail, or rain, or any snow," Joseph of Arimathea, weary of wandering, thrust his staff of hawthorn deep in the ground, where it miraculously took root and bloomed at Christmas time. The thorn tree thus planted still exists, and on this spot was built the first Christian Church in England, if tradition is to be believed.

Joseph of Arimathea and his few followers established the first monastery at Glastonbury, and they mounted guard over the Holy Grail, while preaching the gospel to all the people around them, and converting many by the miracles they wrought. Years passed on, and the sacred vessel remained visible to all the good; but sin having at last appeared even among its chosen guardians, the Holy Grail was carried away by the angels. It had sojourned so long in England, however, that the monarchs of that country were given the highest seat at religious councils in the Middle Ages, and could claim precedence over even the French kings, the avowed champions of the Virgin Mary.

From time to time, some specially favoured mortal was permitted to view the Holy Grail, which plays such an important part in the legends of King Arthur, of Parzival and of Lohengrin, and, as the Holy Grail legend was incorporated in these chivalric romances, it became the theme of poets and minstrels, and was soon familiar to all.[1] In modern times the old legend has been used by Tennyson, in his Idylls of the King, and by Wagner in his last great opera. Mr. Abbey has also availed himself of it for the series of paintings with which he has so beautifully decorated the Boston Public Library.

In the Gospel of Nicodemus, in the apocrypha, we find a detailed account of Christ's three successive trials. While the Bible account forms the real basis of this work, it is adorned by many legends, which have figured in the Miracle plays. But, as the authentic record is so familiar to all readers, we will here give the traditional account only, as it is related in the apocrypha.

The chief priests and scribes, having taken council together, visit Pilate and in his presence make a formal charge against Jesus, saying: "We know this man that he is the son of Joseph the carpenter, born of Mary, and he saith that he is the Son of God and a king; moreover he profaneth the Sabbath and wishes to abolish the law of our fathers."

This accusation is so general, that Pilate inquires more closely into the nature of the

---

[1] See the author's Legends of the Middle Ages, American Book Co.

charges, and in answer to his questions, the angry Jews relate Christ's miraculous cures on the Sabbath-day, accuse Him of being a magician, and especially of driving out demons in the name of Beelzebub. The Roman governor listens contemptuously to all the Jews' denunciations. He soon perceives that there is no real ground for arresting Jesus, and hoping to be able to escape doing so without giving any offence to these prominent men, he asks with simulated innocence: "Tell me how can I, who am a governor, try a king?"

This question provokes a new storm of indignant accusations, and after listening for some time to their protests that the man is not a king, although He claims to be one, Pilate calls one of his officers and sends him to get Jesus, saying: "Let Jesus be brought with gentleness."

The officer, thus instructed, goes out in search of Jesus, and when he comes into the Saviour's presence, he recognizes and worships Him. Then spreading out his scarf or mantle before Him, with the deference he would have shown to a king, he says, "Lord, walk here, and come in, for the governor calleth thee."

The Jews, seeing the outward marks of respect shown to the prisoner by the Roman officer, are indignant; so Pilate, urged by them, asks the officer why he treats Christ with such extreme deference. In answer to this question the officer relates how he saw Christ enter Jerusalem in triumph, and that even the children of the accusers had strewn palms before Him, singing his praises and loudly hailing Him, "King of the Jews." The scribes and high priest, furious at this statement, which they cannot deny, try to confound the officer by asking how he, a Greek, could understand the cries of Hebrew children. But the officer answers that a man standing by had told him that "Hosanna" meant "Save thou, thou that art the highest: Blessed is he that cometh in the name of the Lord."

The Jews, strange to relate, do not object to this explanation, but again insist that Jesus be brought into the council-hall before Pilate. So the officer shows Him in with every outward mark of deepest respect, and as Christ enters the Judgment hall, the standards in the hands of the guards bow down before Him.

The exasperated Jews now loudly accuse the bearers, who vow that the standards bowed down of their own accord, and to test the truth of this statement, Pilate orders that Jesus be taken out of the hall, and twelve strong men selected to hold the Roman banners. The Jews make a careful choice, and six strong men grasp each standard and take up their post on either side of the hall. But when Jesus is again ushered in, the standards, notwithstanding the resistance of the stalwart bearers, bow down as before.

Impressed by this miracle, Pilate hesitates and tries to temporize. He would like to release the prisoner, especially after receiving a written message from his wife, Procla, who, although she has until then been inclined to favour the Jewish religion, now implores her husband not to harm the "Just man," on whose account she has "suffered much in a dream."

The Jews, hearing this, vow that the dream — caused by the prisoner who is well versed in magic — is merely another trick, until Pilate, urged on by them, begins a systematic trial, in which, however, much to their dismay, he carefully investigates all the charges they make against Jesus.

Thus, all those who had been cured on the Sabbath-day are called in, and they one and all testify in favour of the Physician who had made them whole. There is, in the spurious Gospels, a pretence of fair play, and when the Jews bring up the question of Jesus' birth, twelve influential citizens bear witness that they were present at the espousals of Joseph and Mary.

Upon hearing this, Pilate orders the hall cleared, and remaining alone with these twelve witnesses he asks them: "'On what account wish they to slay Him?' They say unto him, 'They are jealous because He healeth on the Sabbath.' Pilate saith, 'For a good work do they wish to slay Him?' They say unto him, 'Yea.'"

Full of wrath which he no longer seeks to conceal, Pilate now goes out to the Praetorium, and taking the sun to witness (in the old Miracle plays, Pilate and Herod always swear by Mahomet, notwithstanding the fact that the prophet was born six centuries after Christ), declares that he can find no fault with this man.

But the Jews are so anxious to secure their ends, that they force him to try the prisoner again. Once more Pilate questions Jesus, who, when asked if He is a king, replies: "'Thou sayest; for I am a king; for this was I born, and I am come that every one who is of the truth should hear my voice.' Pilate saith unto him, 'What is the truth?' Jesus saith unto him 'Truth is from heaven.' Pilate saith, 'Is truth not upon earth?' Jesus saith to Pilate, 'Thou seest how they who say the truth are judged by those who have power upon earth.'"

A second time Pilate acquits Jesus, and now the Jews resort to their last expedient, and accuse Jesus of boastful sacrilege, in regard not only to their temple but to God. To force Pilate to do their will, the priests and scribes proceed to entangle him by subtle logic to acknowledge God above Caesar, and any detractor of Caesar worthy of death. Then, this point being reached, Pilate is driven to give the prisoner a third trial, in which he despairingly asks Him, "'What shall I do to thee?' Jesus saith to Pilate, 'As it hath been given thee.' Pilate saith, 'How has it been given?' Jesus saith, 'Moses and the prophets spake beforehand of my death and resurrection.'" This statement is considered so blasphemous by the Jews, that they clamour more and more fiercely for the prisoner's condemnation and death.

> "He hath blasphemed God!
> We need no witness more.
> Condemned to death
> By law is He;"—
> So rages Sanhedrim.
> *Passion Play at Oberammergau.*

Pilate, dreading their fury, no longer dares resist them, and after again declaring he can find no sin in the prisoner, and publicly washing his hands in token that he is innocent of the crime they are about to commit, he finally gives Jesus up to them to be scourged, and then crucified, in company with two malefactors, Dysmas and Gestas.

CHAPTER IX.

THE CRUCIFIXION.

The willow-tree — The birch-tree — The crown of thorns — Legend of the robin — The roses — Legend of the Cross — Seth's visit to Paradise — Seth's vision — The three seeds — Solomon and the tree — The Queen of Sheba — The pool of Bethesda — The legend of Golgotha — Constantine's cross — Constantine's conversion — Helena's conversion — Helena's dream — The finding of the Cross — The Cross in Persia — Heraclius and the Cross — The Invention of the Cross — The lance of Longinus — The three nails — The cross-bill.

THE apocryphal narrative closely follows the Scripture account of the Crucifixion, and the legends supply only a few curious details in connection with the preparatory tortures undergone by Our Lord. For instance, we are told that the soldiers, after fastening Him to a pillar, raced out into the yard to get switches wherewith to scourge Him, as they had been instructed. A willow-tree was growing in the yard, and its long lithe branches seemed so suited to their purposes, that they took a number of them, and used them for the cruel flagellation.

The men themselves felt no pity, but when the proud tree saw the use to which its slender branches had been put, it no longer held them proudly upright as before, but drooped, and actually shed tears, whence it has ever since been known as the weeping willow. But another legend says that the scourges were taken from a birch-tree, which was thenceforth struck with a blight, and that its descendants are the dwarf birches, so common in many parts of the world.

After the flagellation — so often seen in art, and represented with horrible realism in the mediæval plays — came the mock coronation of Our Lord. Many legends are connected with the crown of thorns, and much discussion has been indulged in concerning the name of the plant which furnished the materials for its manufacture.

There is, in Palestine, a creeping plant called *Spina Christi*. The stems are so flexible that it could easily be "platted," as the Scripture mentions, and its thorns are long and very hard. It is probable that the crown was made of this plant; but one legend claims that the crown was made of the willow, and that, in sorrow at being the cause of pain to the Lord, the tree drooped and wept, and the sharp thorns changed themselves into soft, sad-coloured leaves, that they might never, even involuntarily, cause any more suffering. In Germany, France, and England, it is popularly supposed that the crown, placed upon the head of Our Lord, was woven of branches of the black or white thorn (hawthorn), or the wild rose, whose petals, formerly white, owe their rosy tinge to the blood with which they were dyed as they rested upon His brow. This superstition has given rise to the following charm, which is supposed to prevent any festering in a wound caused by a thorn.

> "Our Saviour was of a Virgin born,
> His head was crowned with a crown of thorn;
> It never cankered or festered at all,
> And I hope in Christ Jesus this never shaull."

The Italians claim that the crown of thorns was made of the barberry, but in the West Indies the people say it was formed out of branches of the cashew-tree, and that since then one of the golden petals of its flowers has been black and blood stained.

Another superstition is that the Robin, seeing Our Saviour on the Cross, and wishing if possible to save Him one pang, pecked off a thorn, and bore it away, dyeing its breast red with the blood of the Lord.

> "Sweet Robin, I have heard them say
> That thou wert there upon the day
> That Christ was crowned in cruel scorn,
> And bore away one bleeding thorn,
> That so the blush upon thy breast
> In shameful sorrow was imprest!"
>
> Bishop DOANE.

Sir John Mandeville says that he saw the crown of thorns in the Holy land, and we are also told that it came first into the possession of Baldwin, second king of Jerusalem, and was then given to Saint Louis, king of France. Barefooted he carried one half of the precious relic from Sens to Paris, where he built the Sainte Chapelle on purpose to receive it. The other half of the crown remained however in Constantinople, where, some say, it had been brought by the empress Helena.

Thorns from the crown of Our Lord have been given to other churches, and all who have seen these holy relics say that the spikes are very long, and just like those of the eastern creeper nabk, or *Spina Christi*.

Another superstition, often alluded to by poets, is that from the blood of Our Lord, which fell to the foot of the cross, the red and pink roses eventually sprang. We are also told that the crown was formed of the hawthorn, when in full bloom, and that the flowers which concealed the sharp thorns were dyed red.

> "Men saw the thorns on Jesus' brow,
> But angels saw the roses."
>
> Mrs. HOWE.

There are, of course, countless legends which center around the cross, most of which are alluded to in noted pictures or in well-known writings. Sir John Mandeville mentions these legends, and while it would be too lengthy a process to relate them in detail, as the old writers loved to do, we here give the outline of the principal one among them.

It seems, that although long driven out of the Earthly Paradise, Adam and Eve still retained a lively recollection of the bliss they had enjoyed there, in the days when they were yet free from the taint of sin. When, in the course of years, Adam grew very old, and felt that he was about to die, he was sorely afraid. As yet he had seen no human being bereft of life, except his beloved son Abel, and although several centuries had passed over his head, and he had endured many hardships, he longed to live on. So he called his son Seth, and bade him go in quest, either of the fruit of life, which grew in the middle of the Garden of

Eden, or of the oil of mercy, which flowed there, so that he might be cured of his sickness and his life be prolonged. Seth hesitated, because he did not know the way to the first abode of mankind, but Adam told him he need but follow the traces of his parents' fleeing footsteps, which were branded deep in the soil.

Thus tracing his way step by step, Seth arrived at last at the gate of the earthly Paradise, where he saw the Cherubim, who held a flashing sword which turned every way. This weapon is hence generally represented in early art as a wheel of fire. As Seth saw that it would be impossible to pass in without the angel's permission, he now humbly made known his errand, and begged that he might be allowed to get the balm for which Adam longed so sorely.

But the angel remained at his post, and after gazing sorrowfully at the pleader, he told him that five long days and half a day (five thousand five hundred years) must elapse before the oil of mercy would fall upon Adam's sinful head.

Seth was greatly disappointed, and was about to turn away, when the angel offered to give him a peep into the Garden which his parents had once inhabited, and which they had forfeited by their disobedience to the divine commands. The third son of Adam had so often heard of the glories of Paradise, that he eagerly availed himself of this proposal, and while the flashing sword stood still for a moment, he gazed eagerly through the open gate.

His delighted eyes rested longest however upon a tree in the center of the garden, whose roots reached down to the nethermost depths of hell, while its branches towered far up into the sky. A later version adds, that upon the topmost bough, he even beheld a beautiful young woman holding a radiant babe in her arms, and as the glance of the Infant rested for one moment upon him, his heart was filled with awe.

A moment later, the flashing sword had resumed its swift rotary motion, and Seth learned from the guardian angel, that the child whom he had seen was the Redeemer, whose coming had been foretold when the curse was pronounced upon Adam and Eve, so many years ago.

Then, the angel stretched out his hand, plucked three seeds from the tree of life, and gave them to Seth, bidding him place them under Adam's tongue, when the latter had breathed his last and was laid to rest in Hebron. Seth went home and carefully carried out the angel's orders.

From the three seeds — nourished by the substance of the corruptible Adam — there soon sprang up three slender trees, which, joining together, in the course of time formed but one trunk, which has always been considered an emblem of the Trinity. This tree grew and spread its mighty branches until Abraham came, and rested beneath its shadow, when he first came into Palestine, led by the voice of God. The wonder-working rods of Moses and Aaron, were both twigs from this marvelous tree, and it is said that the great Jewish lawgiver sweetened the bitter waters of Marah by dropping a bit of its bark into the fountain.

Some authorities declare that Adam had been buried in Lebanon, and that David, charmed with the beauty of the tree which grew on his grave, had it transplanted into his palace gardens at Jerusalem. When Solomon began to build the temple which bore his name, he gave orders that the tree should be cut down, and its wood used in the new construction. But, in spite of Hiram, the architect's, well known skill, the tree could never be utilized, for it always proved too long or too short, too thick or too thin, for the purpose for which it was designed. Furious at this peculiar obstinacy on the part of a mere block of wood, Hiram flung it aside in anger.

Sometime after, a woman (Sibylla the legends call her) came and sat down upon the discarded log. But her clothing took fire as she came in contact with it, and as the flames surrounded her, she wildly prophesied that this piece of wood was destined for the utter destruction of the Jews.

To prevent the repetition of such an accident as the one described above, the log was cast into the brook Cedron, whence the mediæval writers gravely inform us that it drifted down into the Jordan and Dead Sea, and from thence into the Red Sea or Persian gulf! Here it was found by the Queen of Sheba, on her way to pay her memorable visit to Solomon, to test his wealth, wit, and wisdom. This Queen had heard of the king's mania for building, and anxious to offer him a present such as she knew he would appreciate, she had the huge piece of timber fished out of the waters, and brought to Jerusalem, where she solemnly presented it to Solomon.

Another version of the story claims that the log, discarded by Hiram at the time of the building of the temple, was thrown across a stream, where it served as a bridge. When the Queen of Sheba was about to pass over it, she was favoured by a vision of the future, and, rather than tread upon the sacred beam, she kilted up her gown, and waded barefoot through the stream.

The miraculous log was by her order brought to Solomon, who covered it with plates of gold, and set it directly above the door of the temple. Here it remained until Abijah, the great king's grandson, pulled it down for the sake of the gold; and, hoping to conceal what he had done, ordered it buried deep down in the Judean soil.

Many years later the pool of Bethesda was dug on the very spot where the wood lay buried, and the waters owed their curative powers to its presence only. It remained there, unseen, until a few days before the Crucifixion, when it mysteriously rose to the surface, was drawn out and laid on the bank to dry.

The executioners were just seeking a piece of wood from which they could make a cross for the torture of the Nazarene. Christ's sentence had followed so closely upon His arrest, that they had but little time for preparation, so they took the traditional log from which they rudely fashioned the Cross.

Strange to relate, the Cross was planted upon the very spot where the tree had grown so many years before, and tradition says that the men, in digging, came upon Adam's skull,

THE CRUCIFIXION. MICHAEL ANGELO

which they left at the foot of the Cross. Hence the hill was called Golgotha, the place of the skull, and the legend adds that as Our Lord hung upon the Cross, some drops of His blood fell upon the skull of Adam, fulfilling the Cherubim's prophecy. It is on account of this legend, that painters so often represent a skull at the foot of the Cross, and when it is seen there, it is intended to indicate that the power of the Redeemer extends from the beginning of the world, and the first man, to all eternity.[1]

We are told that after the Crucifixion, the Cross of Our Lord, together with the crosses of the two thieves, was hastily buried upon Golgotha. There it remained undisturbed, until the reign of the emperor Constantine, with whom the subsequent part of the legend is intimately connected.

This monarch was on his way to fight his rival Maxentius, in 312 A.D., when all at once, he and his army beheld a luminous cross in the sky, and the words, "By this sign conquer." Constantine, who, at that time, had no idea of the meaning of the Cross, was nevertheless so awed by this phenomenon, that he had a standard made like it. The new ban-

---

[1] See the author's Legends of the Rhine. A. S. Barnes & Co.

ner was called Labarum, and was borne before the emperor in the next battle, where he won a brilliant victory. It has been, and is still, a matter of dispute where this miracle really took place; but we find the inhabitants of Autun, Andernach, Sinzig, Verona, and a few other places, all eager to claim that it occurred near their own town.

Shortly after this victory, Constantine, visited by the frightful disease called leprosy, was told that he could be cured only by bathing in the blood of three thousand small children. The physician who had given this peculiar prescription, was about to order the massacre of the children whom he had collected for this purpose, when the mothers rushed into the emperor's presence and begged that their little ones might be spared. Touched by the anguish of these poor women, the emperor refused to follow the physician's advice, and gave the children back to their mothers, saying: "Far better is it that I should die, than cause the death of these Innocents."

This magnanimous conduct was soon rewarded, for that night St. Peter and St. Paul appeared to Constantine, and bade him send for Sylvanus, bishop of Rome, who would show him a pool where he might wash and be healed. When morning dawned, Constantine sent for Sylvanus, whom his guards had much trouble in finding, for, owing to the constant persecutions, the Christians were all hiding in the catacombs or in caves.

The guards, having finally discovered Sylvanus in a cave near Monte Calvo, led him to Constantine, who described his vision, asking the names of the men he had seen. As soon as he finished, Sylvanus exclaimed that he had evidently been visited by St. Peter and St. Paul, and he produced their effigies, which Constantine immediately recognized.

Sylvanus now began to instruct Constantine, who, hearing of the new religion, became an enthusiastic convert, and begged to be baptized without delay. As the water touched him, he was healed, and gave loud thanks for the miracle which had been worked in his favour. On the very next day he made a decree that Christ should be worshipped as the only God, and that all blasphemers should die. Not content with this demonstration in behalf of the new religion he had embraced, he commanded on the third day that all who insulted Christians should be punished. On the fourth day, Sylvanus, bishop of Rome, was made the first bishop of the world; on the fifth the

Christian Churches were publicly given the right of sanctuaries. The sixth day, Constantine added that no church should be built without the consent of the bishop; on the seventh he gave the domains of Rome to the Church; and eight days after his conversion, he personally began to dig for the foundations of the Lateran Church.

The rumour of Constantine's adoption of the new creed soon spread abroad, and came in time to the ears of his mother Helena, who had joined the synagogue. She boldly professed the ancient Jewish faith, and loudly denounced her son for supporting the Christians. Constantine, wishing to prove to her how mistaken she was, begged her to come to his court with all the most learned rabbis she could find, and there confute the Christians openly.

The result was an august assembly of learned rabbis, who, unable to resist the arguments of Sylvanus, finally had recourse to magic. They sent for a bull, and when one among them had whispered the Jewish name of God in the animal's ear, it fell to the ground dead. The rabbis then triumphantly pointed to it, bidding the spectators recognize the power of a god who could thus slay at a word. Sylvanus, who had listened to their arguments in silence,

VISION OF SAINT HELENA.

now said that if they could restore the animal to life by a word, he would be more ready to believe in the religion they taught. But although the rabbis could kill, they could not restore. Then Sylvanus, stepping up to the dead bull, bade him rise in the name of Christ, and when all the witnesses saw the animal rise up alive, they testified in favour of the new religion, and Helena became a Christian.

She showed her zeal for the new faith by visiting the Holy Land, where she discovered many relics. She also practised the new religion so carefully that she subsequently won the title of Saint, by which she is known in the Roman Catholic Calendar.

Helena's greatest wish, we are told, was to recover the Cross, and when she arrived at Jerusalem she began to search for it with great zeal. Some of the Jews knew that it had been buried on Golgotha, immediately after the Crucifixion, and as they had heard a prophecy to the effect that the Cross would overthrow their religion, they resolved to keep the matter a secret. They therefore bound themselves by solemn oath never to reveal that it lay directly beneath a small temple, which was dedicated to the worship of Venus.

As Helena could not obtain the information

she wanted, she began to torture the Jews, and finally wrung from one of them a promise to reveal the spot where the Cross was buried. Led by this man, Zaccheus, the empress went to Golgotha, and after some search they found the three crosses. But, as Helena did not know upon which Our Lord had suffered, she made several tests of the power of these crosses, and when she found that one of them cured the sick and restored the dead to life, she knew that she had found the object of her pious search. Helena longed to have the three nails also, and after a fervent prayer for their recovery they appeared above ground, bright and shining like gold.

The Cross, thus recovered, was divided into two pieces, one of which was left in Jerusalem, while the other was carried to Rome, where it was placed in a church built on purpose to receive it, and known as the Church of Santa Croce. The empress also carried off the three nails, placed one of them in her son's crown, the second in his horse's bit, and flung the third into the Adriatic. There, it had a miraculous effect upon the whirlpool which had once made this sea most dangerous to mariners, and which now became still.

In the year six hundred and fifteen, the

Persian king Chosroes took Jerusalem, and bore off in triumph the other half of the Holy Cross. He was however soon forced to relinquish this trophy, for Heraclius pursued and defeated him, and brought the relic back to Jerusalem amid general rejoicings. The emperor rode in triumph at the head of his army, but as he drew near to the gates of Jerusalem, he was surprised to see the walls close up by miracle, to prevent his entrance. While he paused astonished, an angel of the Lord appeared to him, saying, " When the King of Heaven and Earth entered through this gate to suffer for the sins of the world, He entered not with regal pomp, but barefooted and mounted upon an ass." Thus rebuked, Heraclius hastily dismounted, removed his crown, royal garments, and footgear, then, taking the Cross upon his shoulders, he marched toward the walls, which now opened of their own accord to let him in. A festival, called the Invention of the Cross, has been celebrated on the third of May ever since the sixth century, to commemorate this recovery of the Holy Cross from the Persians.

From that time until a comparatively recent date, it was customary to preach a sermon to the Jews on that day. All through the Middle Ages, this unfortunate race was driven by force to church on that day, and compelled to hear mass. This compulsion was then considered very praiseworthy, and we find in a sixteenth century diary the following comment upon this custom, which Robert Browning has utilized for a strange poem.

"And a moving sight in truth, this, of so many of the besotted, blind, restive, and ready-to-perish Hebrews, now maternally brought,—nay (for He saith: 'Compel them to come in'), haled, as it were by the head and hair, and against their obstinate hearts, to partake of the heavenly grace."

There is also in Rome, in the same church as the relics of the Cross, the title of accusation, which was also found by Helena. It is a piece of wood, painted white, and the threefold inscription is marked upon it in red letters.

The sponge from which Our Lord tasted the vinegar is also preserved in the church of St. John Lateran, as well as the lance which pierced the Saviour's side, and of which the head is carefully preserved in the Sainte Chapelle in Paris.

We are told that this lance belonged to the Roman Centurion Longinus, who was present at the Crucifixion. He was suffering at that time from an affection of the eyes; but having accidentally touched them with the hand upon which some of the Saviour's blood had fallen, his sight was restored. Converted by this miracle, he went in search of the apostles, who baptized and instructed him; then he proceeded to Cesarea, where his dearest wish was granted and he was allowed to die for his faith.

The lance he wielded, — which some authorities claim was brought to Europe by the returning crusaders in 1098, — plays an important part in some of the legends of the Holy Grail. In the story of Parzival, we find that the cruel wound of Amfortas, which causes him such untold suffering, was inflicted by this holy lance, when he strayed from the path of virtue. His suffering is however ultimately ended by the same means, and in the opera based upon this legend, the lance is a very picturesque feature.[1]

The nails of the Crucifixion, of which the legend speaks, have been said to possess such miraculous powers, that nails made like them, and merely brought into contact with the originals, have been endowed with similar virtues. In connection with the nails we have a beautiful German legend which has been translated as follows by Longfellow: —

[1] See the author's Stories of the Wagner Opera.

"On the cross the dying Saviour
Heavenward lifts his eyelids calm,
Feels, but scarcely feels, a trembling
In his pierced and bleeding palm.

"And by all the world forsaken,
Sees he how with zealous care
At the ruthless nail of iron
A little bird is striving there.

"Stained with blood and never tiring,
With its beak it doth not cease,
From the cross 't would free the Saviour,
Its Creator's son release.

"And the Saviour speaks in mildness:
'Blessed be thou of all the good!
Bear as token of this moment,
Marks of blood and holy rood!'

"And that bird is called the crossbill;
Covered all with blood so clear,
In the groves of pine it singeth
Songs, like legends, strange to hear."[1]

JULIUS MOSEN.

[1] Houghton, Mifflin and Co.

CHAPTER X.

DEATH, BURIAL, AND RESURRECTION OF CHRIST.

The Wandering Jew in fiction — The legend of the Wandering Jew — The Wandering Jew in Europe — The Crucifixion — The seamless coat — The legend of Pilate — The penitent thief — The fallen idols — The descent from the Cross — The Pieta — The entombment — La Pâmoison — The Jews' decision — Joseph imprisoned — Guards at the sepulchre — Joseph missing — The guards' defence — The Ascension — The rumours — The search for Christ — The finding of Joseph — Joseph's account of his escape.

THE next legend, important enough to claim our attention, is that of the Wandering Jew, which appears so frequently in literature, and which has been used in fiction by many authors, among whom are Eugène Sue, F. Marion Crawford, Gen. Lew Wallace and Eugene Field. The last named writer has cleverly identified the old-time story with the Holy Cross Mountain, where he has generously granted the Jew his long-sought-for rest.

There are many versions of this legend, and the Wandering Jew is called Josephus, Isaac

Lakedion, Cartaphilus, or Ahasuerus. He is said to have been only about eight years older than the Christ, and to have been Pilate's porter, or a shoemaker who dwelt near the gate of the city. He belonged to the tribe of Naphtali, and when Jesus, fainting beneath the burden of His cross, fell in front of his door, he struck the Saviour a savage blow with his fist, and roughly said: "Go faster, Jesus, go faster, why dost thou linger?" The Saviour glanced reproachfully at him, and answered: "I indeed am going, but thou shalt tarry till I come."

Some authors claim that the unhappy man, urged on by a power he could not resist, began his endless wanderings at that very moment. Summer and winter, under sun and rain, he journeys on. No danger appals him, sickness and death pass him by, and at the end of each century the Wandering Jew falls into a sort of trance, from which he awakens only to find himself as young as when he thrust the Lord away from his door.

As the plague in the Middle Ages, and the cholera in more recent times, has appeared mysteriously in one place after another, it is a popular superstition that it follows the Wandering Jew wherever he goes, and that it is part of

CHRIST BEARING THE CROSS. (Raphael.)

his awful punishment to leave death and sorrow in his wake.

In Westphalia they declare he can only pause for a short rest in places where he finds two oaks growing in the form of a cross. The Danes say that he rides about on a white horse, uttering dark predictions of future woes, such as battle, murder, or great conflagrations. In Belgium, the Wandering Jew is credited with similar powers, and several persons seriously asserted that they had seen him, even in the last century.

Besides the legends connected with the instruments of the Passion, and the Wandering Jew, tradition has ventured to make very few additions to the account of the Crucifixion as given in the canonical works. Still there are a few details of which artists have made use, and which, on that account, claim a brief notice.

For instance, we are told that Christ's mother, seeing Him bound and helpless, knotted her own veil around Him, when the brutal soldiers had divested Him of the seamless coat for which they cast lots. This latter garment was, however, soon purchased by Pilate. He wore it under his own robes, when summoned to Rome to give an account of himself, after Veronica's handkerchief had cured the Emperor Tiberius of leprosy, as one tradition claims. As long as Pilate wore this garment, the furious Tiberius could do him no harm, and did not even dare to revile him as he wished. But the emperor, having discovered what it was that protected Pilate from his anger, gave orders that the seamless garment should be taken from the ex-governor. Pilate, afraid of retribution, now committed suicide, if one of the versions of the legend is to be believed ; but according to another, he was converted and died a martyr, his wife Procla expiring of joy when she saw his soul, or his head borne up to heaven.

The first legend claims that the virtuous Romans, indignant at Pilate for having condemned Christ to death, flung his body into the Tiber river. The stream shrank with horror from such an accursed man, and overflowing upon the neighbouring country, caused so much damage that the Romans were only too glad to fish Pilate's body out again, and fling it into the sea. The Mediterranean, as anxious to preserve its purity as the Tiber, also refused to cover the body with its waves, and tossed it up on land, where further unpleasant manifestations made it clear that Pilate's tomb was doomed to be a place of turmoil. So the Romans placed the corpse upon a barge, and sent it up the Rhone to Vienne, because they owed the inhabitants of that city a secret grudge. The body, cast into the river there, caused such a commotion that it was taken out, and conveyed to a lonely mountain peak, where it was buried in a little pool.

A third legend claims that Pilate, haunted by remorse, could find no rest. He too became a wanderer upon the face of the earth, and having at last come to a high mountain in Switzerland, he flung himself down from one of its rocky projections, into the Lake of Lucerne below it. It is in memory of this suicide that the mountain still bears his name, and the peasants think that his unhappy ghost still haunts the barren heights of Mount Pilatus.

As Christ hung upon the Cross, with a malefactor on either side of Him, we are told that He remembered the promise made so many years before. So He turned to the merciful thief, and bade him hasten to the gate of Paradise, where the angel would immediately admit him if he only showed the sign of the Cross which he bore upon his shoulders. Another very curious legend states that Our Lord (although nailed to the Cross) wrote a letter which He gave to the repentant thief, bidding him give it to the angel at the gate of Paradise, and assuring him that it would do him good service as a passport.

A third legend, conforming a little more closely with the Scripture narrative, tells us that after making him the solemn promise, "Verily, verily, I say unto thee that to-day thou art with Me in Paradise," Christ bade the thief precede Him to Hades, and there announce His coming to all the dead who had so long awaited their release.

The phenomena attending the Crucifixion, as recorded in the Gospels, are all repeated in the legends, which add that at the Saviour's last cry, "It is finished," the heathen gods gave up their sway, and a mournful voice was heard proclaiming far and near, "Pan is dead." This belief has been embodied in a beautiful poem, by Mrs. Browning, of which only a fragment is given here : —

> "Calm, of old, the bark went onward,
> When a cry more loud than wind,
> Rose up, deepened, and swept seaward,
> From the pilèd Dark behind ;
> And the sun shrank and grew pale,
> Breathed against by the great wail,—
> Pan, Pan is dead.
>
> "And the rowers from the benches
> Fell,— each shuddering on his face,—

While departing Influences
Struck a cold back through the place;
And the Shadow of the ship
Reeled along the passive deep,—
   Pan, Pan is dead.

"And that dismal cry rose slowly
And sank slowly through the air,
Full of spirits' melancholy
And eternity's despair!
And they heard the words it said,—
Pan is dead,— Great Pan is dead,—
   Pan, Pan is dead.

"'T was the hour when One in Sion
Hung for love's sake on a cross;
While His brow was chill with dying,
And His soul was faint with loss;
When His priestly blood dropped downward,—
   Then, Pan was dead.

"Wailing wide across the islands
They rent, vest-like, their Divine!
And a darkness and a silence
Quenched the light of every shrine;
And Dodona's oak swang lonely
Henceforth to the tempest only!
   Pan, Pan was dead."

After the Crucifixion, one of the most frequently used subjects for works of art is the Descent from the Cross. Here again the Scripture account is very brief, but the legends tell us that Joseph of Arimathea, a member of the Sanhedrim, went to Pilate, and in a long and cleverly devised speech, besought permission to bury the body of our Crucified Lord.

Pilate would not at first accede to this request, because he deemed it impossible that Christ should already be dead, but when the centurion confirmed the news, he gave Joseph the required permission. Tradition relates, that besides the Virgin and the faithful women who attended her, John, Nicodemus, and a few others helped Joseph in his pious task.

To save poor Mary every possible pang, John carefully concealed the cruel nails, and when the Lord's body had reverently been taken down from the Cross, it was laid on the Virgin's lap. Then the Virgin once more clasped her beloved Son to her aching heart, which had indeed been pierced by a sword as Simeon had predicted.

This scene, frequently represented in art, and called the Pieta, sometimes includes a host of sorrowful angels, who gaze in reverent awe upon the shattered temple of Our Saviour's body, while a few among them soar heavenward with the emblems of the Passion.

The purification and embalming of the body of Our Lord is also often depicted, and the slab of rock upon which the corpse was laid,

MATER DOLOROSA. (Guido Reni.)

and which is known as the Stone of Unction, is now in the chapel of Calvary, where it is protected by a covering of white marble and surrounded by an iron balustrade.

As the Virgin is supposed by some authorities to have fainted at the sight of the awful suffering of her beloved Son, she is sometimes represented in a swoon as Our Lord passes on to Golgotha, when He is nailed to the Cross, at the moment when His body is lowered, or at the entombment. It is on this account too, that the Church of Rome holds a mournful commemorative service of this pitiful circumstance. All throughout southern Europe this office is held in the Holy Week, and in France it is known as La Pâmoison, or the swoon.

When all was over, and as the sun was rapidly sinking on that awful Good Friday, John, mindful of the charge which he had received, took the Virgin to his own home, which she never left as long as she lived. And, while the small band of faithful mourners sat weeping together, the Jews, having recovered from the terror they had experienced at the miraculous darkness and the violent earthquake which overthrew twenty cities in Asia, again assembled in council. They had heard that the body of Jesus had been given to Joseph of Arimathea for burial, and furious against him and Nicodemus, they expelled them both from the synagogue.

Not content with thus disgracing these two prominent men, they further decided in their anger, that Joseph of Arimathea deserved death. They could not execute him now that the Sabbath was so near, so they had him seized, and imprisoned in a windowless hut, around which they stationed guards, keeping the key, lest they should be deprived of their revenge.

Then, remembering that there had been a rumour among the disciples of the Christ, that He would rise again on the third day, they made Pilate station a guard of five, or five hundred men, at the tomb, before whose opening they placed a ponderous stone which they carefully sealed. Their precautions had been so well taken that they felt it impossible that any trickery should be used, and as soon as the Sabbath was over, early on the third day, they assembled to decide how they should put Joseph of Arimathea to death. As some sort of a trial was indispensable, the high priest gave the key of the prison to one of his satellites, and bade him fetch the delinquent.

A few moments later the man returned, without the prisoner, and crying that although the seals were unbroken, and there was no possible means of egress, the captive had escaped. The Jews were speechless from amazement at first, but even when they had recovered the use of their tongues, they could find no explanation for this mysterious disappearance. They were still wondering where Joseph could have gone, when the guards posted near the tomb of Jesus came into the room. They announced that there had been an earthquake, and that they had seen an angel of the Lord come down from heaven, and roll away the stone from the sepulchre. This account, which is given in the apocrypha, then continues: "And he (the angel) shone like snow and like lightning; and we, being greatly afraid, lay as if we were dead. And we heard the voice of the angel talking with women who waited by the tomb, — ' Fear ye not; for I know that ye seek Jesus who was crucified. He is not here; he is risen, as he said. Come, see the place where the Lord lay; and go forth quickly, and tell his disciples that he is risen from the dead, and is in Galilee.'"

The indignant Jews then inquired why the guards had not laid hands upon the women, and when the soldiers pleaded their fear of the angel, they tauntingly exclaimed: "As the Lord liveth, we do not believe you." This insult proved too much, and the men, whose bearing until then had been quite humble, although they had evidently heard some rumours of Joseph's mysterious escape, now defiantly said: "We have heard that ye shut up him that asked for the body of Jesus, and sealed the door, and when ye opened it ye found him not; therefore produce him that ye kept and we will give up Jesus."

"The Jews said, 'Joseph went away to his own city.' They of the guard said to the Jews, 'And Jesus arose, as we heard from the angel, and is in Galilee.' And the Jews, hearing these words, were greatly afraid, saying, 'Lest this saying should be heard, and all men should believe in Jesus.' And the Jews took counsel together, and took money enough and gave it to the soldiers, saying, 'Say ye, "While we slept his disciples came and stole him. And if this should be heard by the governor, we will assure him and make you safe."' And the soldiers, receiving it, said as they were admonished by the Jews, and their saying was sent abroad among all men."

A few days later three men, Phineas a priest, Aggæus a Levite, and Adas a soldier or teacher, arrived at Jerusalem after a journey in Galilee. They first went to the rulers of the synagogue, and told them that they had seen Jesus sitting on a mountain, which is called Melek, Mamilk, and the Mount of Olives in the different versions of the tale which have come down to us. The man whom the Jews had crucified sat there quietly among His disciples, and the three strangers heard Him say: " Go into all the world and preach to every creature ; he that believeth and is baptized shall be saved, and he that believeth not shall be condemned."

They also reported the Ascension of Our Lord, which they had witnessed, together with about five hundred spectators. Now, in spite of the standing of these three witnesses, the high priest refused to believe their testimony, until they had sworn upon the sacred books that they were telling the truth. Then, fearful lest this news should spread and win new adherents to Jesus, he not only bribed these men to keep silence, but even sent them away secretly to another place.

In spite of all these precautions, the rumour of the Resurrection and Ascension rapidly spread ; and, notwithstanding all that Caiaphas and those whom he had bribed could say, many believed that Jesus was the Son of God. Nicodemus, hoping to strengthen their faith, reminded them that ascensions were not entirely unknown even in their history; seeing that Enoch and Elijah had both gone to heaven without suffering death. He added, that just as the prophets sought for Elijah, notwithstanding Elisha's story, they might now send to Galilee, and make a diligent search for Jesus. This advice pleased the Jews. A search party was organized, and although no trace of the missing Jesus could be found, the messengers came back awestruck, and reported to the rulers that they had discovered Joseph of Arimathea, sitting quietly in his own home.

These tidings were so startling that the High Priest assembled his council, and after much discussion a letter was written, inviting Joseph to come to Jerusalem, and couched in the following terms: "Father Joseph: Peace to thee and to all thine house, and to thy friends. We know that we have offended against God, and against thee, his servant. Therefore we entreat thee to come hither to us thy children: for we have wondered much how thou didst escape from prison, and we truly say that we took evil counsel against thee. But God, who saw that we took unjust counsel against thee, delivered thee out of our hands. Nevertheless, come to us; for thou art the honour of our people."

Seven of Joseph's friends carried this letter to him, and having given him every assurance that he could visit Jerusalem in safety, they escorted him thither. Then, in the presence of the assembled Sanhedrim, Joseph related how, after being locked up, he betook himself to fervent prayer for support and consolation.

He continued thus in supplication all through the Sabbath-day, " And at midnight I saw the prison-house, that four angels lifted it up, holding it by the four corners. And Jesus entered like lightning, and through fear of Him I fell to the ground. Therefore taking me by the hand, He raised me, saying; ' Fear not, Joseph!' Then He embraced and kissed me, and said, 'Turn and see who I am.' Therefore I turned and looked and said, ' Lord, I know not who thou art.' He saith, 'I am Jesus, whom thou didst bury the day before yesterday.' I said to Him, 'Show me the sepulchre, and then I will believe!' Therefore He took me by the hands and led me away to the sepulchre which was open. And when I saw the linen clothes and the napkin, and knew, I said, ' Blessed is He that cometh in the name of the Lord,' and worshipped Him. Then He took me by the hand, the angels also following, and led me to Arimathea to my house, and saith unto me. 'Abide here for forty days. For I go unto My disciples that I may instruct them to preach My resurrection.'"

In another version of this book of the apocrypha, Joseph states that he fainted at the sight of the Lord, and recovered his senses only when a great quantity of water had been poured upon him, and a smell of myrrh came to his nostrils.

The members of the Sanhedrim who had listened to his narrative with wonder, were now filled with great fear, and fasted and mourned until Joseph bade them be of good cheer. They remembered the prediction of Simeon; but not quite satisfied by the testimony of Joseph, they again sent for the three men who had witnessed the ascension, and began to question them once more. To make sure that there was no deception practised upon them, the men were cross-questioned separately, but their accounts tallied so closely that there could be no doubt of their really having seen the event they described.

CHAPTER XI.

THE DESCENT INTO HADES.

The sons of Simeon — The Jews ask for their account — The writing of their statement — The dead in Hades — The Light — The prophecies — The plans of Hades and Satan — The story of Lazarus — The defence of Hades — The King of Glory — The entrance of Christ — The submission of Hades — Satan bound — The righteous delivered — Christ appears to Mary — Christ appears to James — Christ leads the redeemed to Paradise — Enoch, Elijah, and the good thief — The two versions — Pilate sees report — Herod's letter — The doom of Herodias — The death of Herod — The death of Pilate.

AFTER these proofs the Jews could no longer doubt the resurrection of Jesus. So Joseph of Arimathea told them that not only had Jesus risen from the dead, but that He had raised others also; and he mentioned among others Karinus and Leucius, the sons of Simeon, who were well known among the Jews. Many of them had even been present at the death and burial of these two men; and when they heard that they were even then living in their own house at Arimathea, they resolved to go in search of them, after ascertaining that their sepulchre was really empty.

Annas, Caiaphas, Joseph, Nicodemus, and Gamaliel, with a few others, were chosen for this embassy, and hastened to Arimathea, where they entered the synagogue, and had the two men in question brought into their presence. Then the high priest, addressing them, said, "We wish you to swear by the God of Israel, and Adonai, and thus that ye may tell the truth how ye rose, and who raised you from the dead!"

The sons of Simeon, who had not uttered a word, now crossed themselves, made signs asking for writing materials, and, locked up in separate cells, wrote the following narrative. This account is very important, because it served as foundation for the Miracle Plays. In England it was known as the Harrowing of Hell, but on the Continent it was called the Descent into Hades. It has also been the basis of a number of paintings by the early masters.

The introduction to these documents, given in full in the apocryphal Gospel of Nicodemus, is as follows: "O Lord Jesus Christ, the resurrection and the life of the world, give us

The Descent into Hades.

grace that we may rehearse Thy resurrection, and Thy wonderful works which Thou didst in Hades."

Karinus and Leucius then went on to relate that they were in the dark depths of Hades with all those who had fallen asleep in the beginning. They were closely watched by Hades himself, Satan, his emissary, and the many demons which guarded the place of the departed spirits.

Great excitement reigned in the dismal precincts of Hades, for John the Baptist had already come thither, to announce their coming release to the weary, waiting souls. The patriarchs and prophets, who had been longing for the time of deliverance, crowded around John in the gloom, when they heard him raise his well-known cry " Repent ye."

Suddenly, "at the hour of midnight, upon those dark places, there arose as it were the light of the sun." This light came streaming down the pathway to Hades, growing brighter and brighter. When its beams allowed them to distinguish one another's faces, the patriarchs and prophets recognised each other, and the latter now solemnly repeated the prophecies which are recorded in their books.

Isaiah in particular exclaimed: "The land of Zebulon and the land of Nephthalim, the people which sitteth in darkness hath seen a great light." Then Simeon related how he had first seen the dawning of the promised light, when the Christ Child had been brought into the Temple, and he had been filled with the Holy Ghost.

At the request of Adam, Seth told the waiting people how he had gone to the gates of Paradise, where the angel had shown him the tree of life, and given him the miraculous seeds. These were to produce a tree which five thousand five hundred years later would bear strange fruit, from whence the oil of mercy would flow for all. Seth's story filled the hearts of the righteous with ineffable joy, and they all anxiously watched the light, which was growing brighter and brighter. While the good were thus revelling in joyful anticipations, "Satan, the inheritor of darkness," was in close confabulation with "Hades, the all devouring and insatiate one." He told him that from the hated race of the Jews there had recently sprung a man, named Jesus, who claimed to be the Son of God. The Jews, through his (Satan's) machinations had grievously persecuted and shamefully put to death this same Jesus, after He had resisted all Satan's most clever temptations.

Hades shrank with fear when he heard of the

coming into his abode of One who said that He was the Son of God. He therefore angrily asked why Satan was bringing Him thither to undo them all. Satan tried to reassure Hades, and repeatedly asserted that Christ was nothing but a man, for he had heard Him exclaim "my soul is exceeding sorrowful unto death."

To convince Hades, Satan began to enumerate all his causes of complaint against Christ, who had healed the sick, restored the blind, and especially cast out the devils purposely sent to torment the human race. The greatest of all his grievances, however, was that Christ had snatched from his grasp certain dead persons, and restored to life those whom he had hoped to detain in Hades forever.

Satan concluded his speech by a passionate plea to Hades to use all his power to keep Christ a prisoner when He came, as come He must, into his dark abode. But Hades doubtfully shook his head, and said, "A short time ago I swallowed a certain dead man, Lazarus by name, and a little after, one of the living, by a word alone, forcibly drew him out of my bowels."

Not content with this statement, which must have been explicit enough to suit the taste of the times, Hades now went on to describe his sensations on that occasion; and he ruefully commented upon the fact that Lazarus flew away from him "not like a dead man but like an eagle." Shrewdly suspecting that Lazarus had been called forth by the very man whom Satan now bade him detain at any price, Hades refused to let Christ enter his realm, lest if once admitted there He should rob him of the dead, and annul his power forever.

At the end of a lengthy discussion, Satan and Hades concluded to bar all their gates; but when that was done, a mighty voice was heard without, crying, "Lift up your gates, O ye rulers, and be ye lifted up, eternal gates, and the King of Glory shall come in."

Afraid lest the very gates should fall at this cry, Hades urged Satan to rush out at the head of the demoniac forces, while he and the other demons tried to reinforce their defences. The righteous, hearing the orders given by Hades for resistance, now warned him that his efforts would all be vain, for Isaiah and Hosea had both predicted many years before that, "The dead shall arise, and they that are in the tombs shall be raised, and those who are in the earth shall be glad. And where is thy sting, O Death? Where is thy victory, O Hades?"

Just then the voice without was again heard

DESCENT INTO HADES.

asking for admittance ; and, hoping to temporise, Hades began to parley, and craftily inquired, "Who is the King of Glory?" The question was no sooner asked than it was answered by a triumphant burst of music from the heavenly host, who loudly proclaimed Him: "The Lord strong and mighty, the Lord mighty in battle."

As the walls of Jericho fell of old at the sound of the sacred trumpets, so the gates of Hades now burst asunder at this triumphant cry, and the bonds of all the dead were loosened. They sprang forward, with a cry of rapture, to greet on the threshold the King of Glory, who entered, holding aloft His banner, which bore the emblem of the Cross.

All the dark corners of Hades were lighted up by His presence, and revealed all the grimacing and vindictive fiends which the ancients loved to depict and describe. Some artists have even gone so far, when treating this subject, as to represent Christ stepping over the door, which has fallen upon Hades, who is crushed flat beneath its weight.

The light which emanated from the Saviour flooded the little group of patriarchs and prophets, who fell upon their knees and worshipped Him.

Another version of the Descent into Hades says that Christ was preceded by the repentant thief, bearing his cross, and announcing the coming of his Master. Hades, terrified at the entrance of Christ, hastened to do homage to the Lord, with all his demon crew; and Christ, after bidding His angels bind Satan, the traitor, delivered him over into Hades' keeping, saying, "Take him and keep him safely until my second coming."

In his wrath against Satan, who by compassing the death of Christ robbed him so sorely, Hades condemned him to the worst tortures, and bitterly reproached him, saying, "All that thou didst gain by the tree of knowledge, thou hast lost it all by the tree of the Cross."

In the mean while Christ had graciously stretched out His right hand and raised Adam, in sign of complete forgiveness. Then addressing the righteous, whom Adam gazed at in wonder, questioning whether they could all have descended from him, the Saviour said, "Come with me all ye who have died through the tree which he touched. For behold I raise you all up again through the tree of the Cross."

All the blessed then returned loud thanks for the mercy vouchsafed them, and, before leaving Hades forever, they implored the Lord to set up

His banner there in token of His everlasting victory over the powers of sin and death.

"And when they had said these things, the Saviour blessed Adam on the forehead with the sign of the Cross, and He did this also to the patriarchs and the prophets, and martyrs and forefathers, and took them, and sprang out of Hades. And as He went the holy fathers followed Him, chanting and saying, "Blessed is He that cometh in the name of the Lord. Alleluia; to Him be glory from all the saints."

The dead, thus released, were led first of all into the presence of the Virgin Mary. She was sorrowing, and knelt in her house at that time, saying: "Thou didst promise, O my most dear Son, that Thou wouldst rise again on the third day. Before yesterday was the day of darkness and bitterness; and behold, this is the third day. Return then to me, Thy mother, O my Son, tarry not, but come." A very old carol voices this promise of Christ to His beloved mother in the quaint lines:—

> "Upon Easter day, mother,
> My uprising shall be;
> O the sun and the moon, mother,
> Shall both rise with me."
>
> *The Cherry-Tree Carol.*

Mary's prayer was scarcely ended when the room was suddenly flooded by a brilliant light. Then the angelic host appeared, singing a hymn of joyful thanksgiving, and a moment later Jesus entered, bearing the banner of the Cross, and closely followed by the long procession of ransomed souls. They, one and all, knelt before the Virgin Mother, humbly thanking her, through whom their deliverance had at last come.

Sight alone was not enough to convince the bewildered Virgin that it was really her Son. She longed to hear once more His beloved voice, and her joy was complete, therefore, only when He addressed her, saying, " I salute thee, O my mother."

Although this version claims that Christ appeared first of all to Mary, according to another He began by visiting James, who, at the Last Supper, had vowed that he would not taste food again until he had seen the risen Lord. James was well-nigh fainting from exhaustion, by this time, so Christ, appearing to him, urged him to eat, blessing and breaking the food which was set before them, and even partaking of it with him.

A third version relates that Christ, upon leaving Hades, proceeded directly to Paradise, followed by about twelve thousand just men, whom He had released from Hades. There He delivered Adam and his progeny to the archangel Michael, who led them through the gates, into the garden of Eden. To their astonishment they saw two men quietly walking about there.

The holy fathers were so amazed by this sight that they breathlessly asked, "Who are ye, who have not seen death, and have not descended into Hades, but inhabit Paradise in body and soul?" The men then informed them that they were Enoch and Elijah; and that although translated hither in the flesh, it was to be their privilege to go forth and fight the Antichrist. They would be slain in this encounter; but after three days they would rise again and be "caught up in the clouds to meet the Lord."

Enoch and Elijah had scarcely finished this explanation when the righteous beheld a third figure coming to meet them. It was a lowly man, bearing either a cross, or the sign of a cross, upon his shoulders. In answer to the inquiries of the holy fathers, this man now gave his biography, concluding with his conversion upon the cross, and the promise then made to him by Jesus Christ.

Two of the redeemed, Karinus and Leucius, were sent to earth by the archangel Michael, with instructions to preach the resurrection, whenever the Spirit moved them. The remainder of the time they were to be dumb, until the Lord bade them make known all they had heard and seen.

Such was the account of the descent into Hades, penned by Karinus and Leucius in their separate cells. They had begun their task simultaneously, and at the same moment they wrote the last word, and cried aloud, " Amen." Their documents, handed over to the high priest, were carefully compared, and found exactly alike; but when the Jews would fain have questioned these witnesses further, they had vanished, and were never seen again.

The rumour of this report made by these two men finally reached the ears of Pilate, in spite of the precautions which the Jews had taken to keep it secret, and he insisted upon seeing it. When he had read it all, Pilate called the rabbis together, and made them acknowledge that it agreed with the prophecies inscribed in their sacred books.

They said that even the period of five thousand five hundred years, mentioned by Seth, had been plainly indicated by God to Moses when He ordered, "'Make thee the Ark of the Covenant two cubits and a half in length, one cubit and a half in breadth, and a cubit and a half in height.' By these five cubits and a half we understood and knew the frame of the ark of the old covenant, that in five thousand five hundred years Jesus Christ should come in the ark of the body, and we find that He is the God of Israel, the Son of God!"

To avoid dissension in the synagogues, the Jews, nevertheless, resolved to be silent, and prevailed upon Pilate not to reveal what they had told him to any one except the emperor. In the apocrypha we have therefore pretended letters from Pilate to Claudius, as well as some curious communications from Herod to Pilate. In one of these, the former relates a peculiar accident which has just happened to his daughter Herodias. As she "was playing upon a pool of water which had ice upon it, it broke under her, and all her body went down, and her head was cut off and remained on the surface."

This catastrophe, which was considered a judgment upon her for having asked the head of John the Baptist, is not the only mention made of her in the legends. We also find her subjected to the same punishment as the Wandering Jew, of whom she catches a glimpse once in every century, but only across some impassable chasm or stream. They see and recognise each other, stretch out longing arms, and would fain embrace one another, for their common doom has drawn them strangely together, and keeps them constantly conscious of each other, although apart. But they are doomed only to catch this passing glimpse of one another, and ere they can exchange a single word, they are both swept onward by a force which it is impossible to resist.

In his letters, Herod then goes on to confess that punishment is fast overtaking him for his manifold crimes. He confesses that he was the instigator of the Massacre of the Innocents, that he ordered the beheading of John the Baptist, and the scourging of Christ, although history ascribes the first of these crimes to another king of the same name. Punished in the person of his wife, sons, and daughter, Herod is further affected by dropsy, has wept himself blind, and concludes by asking Pilate to bury his unfortunate body, which is already a prey to worms, for "lo, I am receiving temporal judgment, and I am afraid of the judgment to come."

Pilate answers this letter by a stilted production, in which he declares he is innocent of having shed the blood of Christ, and relates the latter's resurrection and apparition in Galilee.

He adds that Procla believes in Him, for she has gone to see Him, together with Longinus, the centurion who pierced Him with his lance, and the guards who watched at the sepulchre.

Pilate himself, according to this version, is favoured by a vision of the risen Saviour, and, kneeling before Him, the proud Roman makes the curious confession : " I have sinned, O Lord, in that I sat and judged Thee, who avengest all in truth. And lo, I know that Thou art God, son of God, and I beheld Thy humanity and not Thy divinity. But Herod, with the children of Israel, constrained me to do evil unto Thee. Have pity, therefore, upon me, O God of Israel."

Another account states that when Pilate was summoned to Rome, tried and condemned for having sentenced Christ, he exclaimed that his punishment was just. His repentance and conversion were so complete, that he is represented as having died like a martyr, comforted at the last moment by a voice from heaven, which addressed him, saying : " All generations, and the families of the Gentiles, shall call thee blessed, because under thee were fulfilled all these things that were spoken by the prophets concerning me ; and thou thyself must appear as my witness at my second coming when I shall judge the twelve tribes of Israel, and them that have not confessed my name."

CHAPTER XII.

ASSUMPTION AND CORONATION OF THE VIRGIN.

Mary at the Ascension — The seven sorrows of the Virgin — Pentecost — The Holy Ghost — Disciples take leave of the Virgin — The Annunciation — The palm — The disciples — Mary's farewell — The Virgin's soul — The shrouding of the Virgin — The funeral of the Virgin — The High Priest — The burial of the Virgin — The Assumption — Thomas' doubts — The girdle — The Coronation — The privilege granted to Mary — The last Judgment.

THE Ascension of Our Lord was witnessed by the Virgin Mary, as well as by the disciples, and the five hundred men whom the three travellers had seen assembled on Mount Melek. Here again the Scripture narrative consists of only a few words, and Mary is not mentioned by name. The legends, however, add sundry details, and tell us that as Jesus soared upward out of her sight, Mary cried aloud in anguish, "My son, remember me when Thou comest in Thy kingdom! Leave me not long after Thee, my Son!"

Assumption and Coronation of the Virgin. 231

This was the last of the Virgin's seven sorrows, which are often represented in art as a series, and include the Circumcision, or the Prophecy of Simeon, the Flight into Egypt, the loss of the Christ Child, the procession to Calvary, the Crucifixion, the Entombment, and the Ascension. The Ascension of Christ having taken place, John took Mary home with him. She lingered in Jerusalem with the disciples, waiting for the promised Comforter, which the Christians interpret to mean the Holy Ghost, while the Mohammedans insist that Christ designated their Prophet by this term.

Mary was not only with the disciples, but she "continued with them in prayer and supplication" until the Day of Pentecost, when the Holy Ghost fell upon her also according to some authorities. But other commentators state that Mary, as the personification of wisdom and mother of divine wisdom, had no need of an increase of knowledge, and that the Holy Ghost had always been with her.

Some legends of great antiquity inform us that Mary was baptised by Peter, and received the Holy Communion from the hands of John, the beloved disciple of Christ. It is not known how Mary spent the remaining years of her life. One tradition claims that she remained at Jerusalem, where she spent all her time in devotion, and in making pious pilgrimages to the places hallowed by Our Saviour's Crucifixion and Entombment. A second report is that she withdrew to a sanctuary which Elijah had built in her honour on Mount Carmel. There she lived the life of a recluse, and hence is known as Our Lady of Carmel and the special patroness of Carmelite nuns. A third version of the story, however, says that she accompanied John to Ephesus, where she dwelt in his house, instructing his many converts, who were all anxious to see and hear the mother of their new-found Lord and Redeemer.

Shortly after the Descent of the Holy Ghost, which is frequently represented in art, the disciples left Jerusalem, in obedience to the instructions of Christ to go forth and preach the gospel to all nations. Before they departed, however, they all came to take solemn leave of the Virgin Mary, and to receive her blessing, for they never expected to see her again upon earth. On this occasion they each spoke a few words, which, joined together, now form the Apostles' Creed.

The date of the death of the Virgin Mary is very uncertain, and while some writers claim that she died in the forty-eighth year of our era,

Assumption and Coronation of the Virgin. 233

others are found to assert that this event took place in the year sixty-three. It is generally supposed though, that the Virgin lived only about eleven years after the ascension.

Although we have no authentic account of her last moments upon earth, there are many legends about her death, which have been generally adopted by artists, and which were accepted with unquestioning faith in the Middle Ages, by the uninstructed classes.

One of these legends is contained in an apocryphal work entitled the "Assumption of the most glorious Virgin Mary," and when condensed it runs as follows: The Virgin was dwelling on Mount Sion, in John's house, eagerly awaiting the moment when she would be allowed to join her beloved Son, whose memory was ever present to her mind. One day her heart was filled with such a weary longing for Him, that she burst into tears and wept abundantly. All at once an angel appeared before her, clothed in radiant garments, and flooding all the house with a dazzling light. Like the Angel of the Annunciation, who had appeared to her so many years before, this angel saluted her saying, "Hail, O Mary!" and then went on to say "Blessed by Him who hath given salvation to Israel! I bring thee here a branch of palm gathered in Paradise; command that it be carried before thy bier in the day of thy death; for in three days thy soul shall leave thy body and thou shalt enter Paradise where thy Son awaits thy coming."

The palm, which the death angel bore, instead of the lily borne by the angel of the Annunciation, was, we are told, an offshoot of the fortunate tree which had sheltered Mary and her Babe during the flight, and which had received the reward of being transplanted into Paradise.

Mary then asked the name of the celestial messenger, besought permission to see the apostles once more before her demise, and asked that they might be present at her death and burial. She also begged that her soul, freed from the body, might not be affrighted by any spirit of darkness, or any demon have power over her.

The angel then informed her that he was called the Great and Wonderful; but another legend adds that he was Raphael. He had been allowed to summon Mary to heaven, in compensation for having been selected, in centuries gone by, to forbid Adam and Eve to eat of the fruit of the tree of the knowledge of good and evil. The angel promised Mary that her request should be granted, and that the twelve disciples should be brought to her from the ends of the earth, in order to receive her last messages and commit her body to the grave. He also quieted her apprehensions, by telling her she need not fear the evil spirit, for her seed had bruised his head, and put an end to his malignant reign.

Then the heavenly visitor departed, leaving behind him the celestial palm, which shed light from every leaf, and sparkled as brightly as the stars of the morning. Left alone once more, Mary lighted her lamp, prepared her bed, and then lying down upon it, and composing herself, she calmly and prayerfully awaited the end.

The disciples were, by this time, scattered far and wide, but at the same moment, John at Ephesus, Peter at Antioch, and all the brethren wherever they happened to be, were suddenly caught up and whisked through the air, like the prophet Habakkuk in the Old Testament. A moment later they were amazed to find themselves all together once more, and standing at the door of Mary's house at Jerusalem. They went in, and when the Virgin saw them standing around her bed, she blessed and thanked them for coming, and explained why they had been summoned thither in such haste. Then she took the palm, and gave it to John, bidding him carry it before her at her burial.

Time passed quickly in praise and prayer, and when the third hour of the night had come on the appointed day, a mighty noise was heard, and a delightful fragrance filled the whole house. According to one version, the archangel Saint Michael now appeared, with all the heavenly host, to receive Mary's soul; but another states that Christ Himself came, accompanied by angels, patriarchs and prophets, all singing loud hymns of joy.

When their grand chorus was ended, Christ tenderly addressed His mother in the words of the Song of Songs, saying, "Arise, my beloved! mine elect! come with me from Lebanon, my espoused! receive the crown that is destined for thee!" Mary gazed upon His beloved face in rapture and answered, "My heart is ready, for it was written that I should do Thy will!"

Then, while all the angels who accompanied the Lord again sang their hymn of joy, Mary's soul, in the guise of a little child, left her body, and was received into the arms of her Son. And behold "the Apostles saw that her soul was such that no mortal tongue could express

ASSUMPTION OF THE VIRGIN. (Titian.)

its whiteness." Still escorted by the heavenly host, Christ now rose up to heaven again, tenderly carrying the released soul of the Virgin Mary.

The apostles, looking upward and seeing her fast vanishing out of their sight, then cried aloud to her, saying: "Oh, most prudent Virgin, remember us when thou comest to glory," while the angels surrounded her, chanting, "Who is this that cometh up from the wilderness, leaning upon her Beloved? she is fairer than the daughters of Jerusalem."

Mary's soul had entirely disappeared from earthly sight, but the disciples gazed with respect upon the empty temple of her body, which still lingered upon earth. As the burial could not long be postponed, however, they soon called the maidens, who came to wash and shroud the corpse of the Virgin. But although they tenderly performed their office, these women were not allowed to gaze upon the body which had borne our Lord, for it was enveloped in such a glory of dazzling light that they could not see it.

Now, while some writers have expressed a belief that Mary did not die, but merely slept, the majority assure us that she was really dead, when the disciples reverently laid her body upon a bier, and proceeded slowly toward the valley of Jehoshaphat where they intended to bury her. John walked ahead of the little funeral procession, carrying the heavenly palm; Peter slowly chanted the one hundred and fourteenth Psalm; while the other disciples and many angels softly took up the strain. The sound of this music attracted the attention of the Jews; and the high priest rushed out in anger, and laid his hand upon the bier, intending to overthrow it. But as he touched it, both his arms fell paralysed along his sides. Terrified by this accident, he now implored Peter to restore them. So Peter gravely said: " Have faith in Jesus Christ and His mother, and thou shalt be healed."

The high priest, converted by the miracle which had just occurred, now openly confessed his belief in Christ and the Virgin Mary, and as soon as he had done so his arms were made whole. Then, the interrupted funeral service went on, and Mary's body was laid in a tomb, near which the disciples kept guard for some time.

Three days after the death of His Virgin mother, Christ spake to the assembled angels, saying: " What honour shall I confer on her who was my mother on earth and brought me forth?" The angelic host unaminously answered: "Lord, suffer not that body which was Thy temple and Thy dwelling to see corruption; but place her beside Thee on Thy throne in heaven." Well pleased with this answer, the Lord bade the angel Michael bring the glorious soul of Mary into His presence, and then He said: "Rise up, my dove, my undefiled, for thou shalt not remain in the darkness of the grave, nor shalt thou see corruption."

At these words the soul of Mary joined her body, and, joyfully obeying the summons she had received, the Virgin arose from her tomb, all glorious without and within. Thus she ascended up into heaven, surrounded by the heavenly choir, which welcomed her with every demonstration of extravagant joy.

The apostles, still mounting prayerful guard around the tomb, witnessed the Virgin's Assumption, which they related to Thomas, the only one among them who had not been present at the time when it occurred. But Thomas would not believe them; and as he insisted upon ocular demonstration, they opened the tomb in which Mary's body had been laid, and showed him that it contained nothing but roses and lilies which breathed forth celestial perfume. Gazing upward, as if in search of the vanished

Mary, Thomas now beheld her in a glory of light; and as she slowly rose to heaven, she threw down to him the girdle which is still preserved as a relic in the cathedral of Prato. The miracle of the Assumption, and of the Girdle, said to have been witnessed by many besides the apostles, is the subject of a number of very noted paintings.

Only one more honour remained to bestow upon Mary. She was crowned "Queen of Heaven," in the midst of the assembled angels. Father, Son, and Holy Ghost participated in this ceremony; and painters, in depicting the Coronation of the Virgin, show her receiving the diadem either from the hands of God the Father, or from God the Son. On this solemn occasion, Mary ventured to make the following request, which causes her still to be viewed in the light of an intercessor by many Christians.

"Do Thou bestow Thine aid upon every man calling upon, or praying to, or naming the name of Thine handmaid." Christ answered: "Every soul that calls upon thy name shall not be ashamed, but shall find mercy and support and confidence both in the world that now is, and in that which is to come, in the presence of My Father in the heavens."

The religious plays of the Middle Ages, and

CORONATION OF THE VIRGIN.

the series of pictures intended to cover all the space between the Downfall of the Angels and the End of the World, set before the eyes of the public the principal scenes of the Old and New Testaments and the apocrypha, and complete the story by a representation of the Last Judgment. The most famous of all the paintings treating of this subject is Michael Angelo's magnificent decoration of the Sistine chapel, where the Virgin seems to shrink from the terrible wrath of her Son. In other pictures, she seems to plead in behalf of guilty humanity; and in some cases she generously screens the sinners behind the folds of her outstretched robe.

CHAPTER XIII.

MOTHER AND SON IN ART.

Christ the model man — Mary the model woman — Christ in early Christian art — The symbols by which He was represented — Pagan and Biblical types of Christ — The Good Shepherd — The Virgin in early art — The disputes and schisms in the Church — The first portrait of the Virgin — John of Damascus — The influence of the Crusades — Saint Bernard's vision — The Church plays — The influence exerted by the Renaissance — The symbols of Mary — The legend of the rose — The names of Mary — The vesture of Mary and Christ — The Madonnas — Our Lady of the Snow — Our Lady of Loretto — Our Lady of the Pillar — Our Lady of the Chair — Series of pictures — The Incoronata — The Mater Dolorosa — The Pieta — The Mater Amabilis — Plants connected with Christ — Plants connected with Mary — Conclusion.

FROM the very first, Christians have ever considered Christ as the model of manly virtue, and before long they also recognised His mother as the pattern woman. All sects have always been ready to acknowledge the Virgin as blessed among women; but while some of the Protestants limit themselves to this recognition, there have always been many Christians who place her above the angels and next to the Trinity. They ascribe to her almost unlimited influence, and therefore address prayers to her as well as to the Deity.

It is not positively known when this worship of the Virgin — which some writers term Mariolatry, first began. There is, however, an authentic mention of invocation to her in the fourth century, and it is probable that the custom had already been in practice for some time.

A remnant of the old Jewish belief, that it was a sin to make likenesses of any living being, together with a feeling of intense reverence for the Saviour, at first prevented any attempt to represent Him except by symbols. The lineaments of the transfigured, risen, and ascending Lord were, besides, so different from His human presentment, that the early Christians preferred to indicate Him by the initial letters of His name, or by such symbols as the Cross, the Lamb, and the Fisherman.

Later on, they indicated Him by pagan allusions; and, because Christ drew all people to Him by the magic of His words, they represented Him as Orpheus, the mythical singer whose lyre attracted all creatures to his side. The next stage in art was to represent Christ by types taken from the Old Testament, where, for instance, Abraham's sacrifice was a foreshadowing of the great atonement to come.

The third step was to depict Our Lord as the Good Shepherd; and while at first He is represented as carrying a sheep, He was in time shown with a kid on His shoulder, to indicate that He had come to bring back into the fold the sinners who were always typified as goats.

> "'He saves the sheep, the goats he doth not save!'
> So spake the fierce Tertullian; but she sigh'd —
> The infant Church! Of love she felt the tide
> Stream on her from her Lord's yet recent grave.
> And then she smiled; and in the catacombs,
> On those walls subterranean, where she hid
> Her head mid ignominy, death, and tombs,
> With eyes suffused, but heart inspired true,
> She her Good Shepherd's hasty image drew,
> And on His shoulders not a lamb, a kid."
>
> MATTHEW ARNOLD.[1]

As persecution and death surrounded the early Christians on all sides, and the insecurity of life made them feel particularly close to the Lord, they dwelt more upon the idea of His divinity and glorification, than upon His humanity and sufferings. It is probably on this account that all real knowledge of the

[1] Macmillan & Co.

physical appearance of Our Lord is lost; although we find in the apocrypha the already quoted document of Lentulus. But it was only in the year one thousand, when all hearts were filled with apprehension of the End of the World, which had been fixed for that date by the superstitious people, that Christians first began to dwell upon the awful scenes of the Last Judgment, and to represent the events of Passion Week, emphasizing the suffering and horror as much as possible.

Whereas Christ in early art had been represented mostly by symbols, the Virgin Mary soon occupied a prominent place in art, and the majority of the church paintings and ornaments were used to set forth her perfections, relate her story, or recommend her to the veneration of the people.

As we have seen, there is but little mention of Mary in the canonical works; but her name came into great prominence when various sects in the Church began to question whether she were mother of the human element only in Christ's nature, or also of the divine. Nestorius maintained the former opinion, and found so many Christians ready to oppose him and his followers, that disputes on the subject were the order of the day.

The matter was finally brought up before the Ecumenical Council at Ephesus in 431, and after much discussion Mary was officially proclaimed the mother of the God, as well as of the man, and as such commended to the worship of all true Christians. This decision occasioned a schism in the Church, and as outward sign of their convictions, the Orthodox, as they were then called, or partisans of the Virgin, made effigies of the Mother and Child, which they placed in their churches and homes, stamped on their coin, and embroidered on their garments.

Not long after the council at Ephesus, the Empress Eudoxia visited the Holy Land, and sent home a portrait of the Virgin and Child, which was supposed to have been painted from life by Saint Luke. This precious work of art was placed in a church at Constantinople, where Mary's remains were also brought in 710. Some authorities claim that Eudoxia's portrait of the Virgin was destroyed by the Turks when they took Constantinople in 1453; but the Venetians declare that it was brought to their city, in 1204, by their blind Doge Dandolo, and placed in the church of St. Mark, where it can still be seen.

During the sixth and seventh centuries, the

worship of the Virgin Mary rapidly increased, and her effigies became so numerous that in the eighth century a reaction set in. Under the pretext that these images no longer served merely as symbols, but were worshipped as idols, a sect called the Iconoclasts, or Image Breakers, began a general destruction of these works of art. Opposition, as usual, only served as stimulus to their zeal; and they forcibly removed from the churches all works of art that did not represent Christ alone.

Statues were broken, paintings burned, mosaics shattered, and thus the principal result of this movement was to deprive posterity of many curious examples of early Christian art. In the Council of Nice in 787, a vehement protest was made against this general destruction, but although checked for a while, it was soon renewed.

In connection with the Iconoclasts, we find that John of Damascus was one of the most zealous defenders of the images of the Virgin. He once protested so vehemently against the destruction of a painting representing her, that the Image Breakers called him an idolater, and as such condemned him to lose his right hand. Tradition adds that they hewed it off on the spot, and that John of Damascus, falling upon his knees, touched the bleeding stump of his hand to the lips of the image he had suffered so intensely to save. He had no sooner touched the pictured Virgin, however, than a miracle occurred, and a new hand sprang up instead of the one which he had lost. It is in commemoration of this miracle, — which naturally filled the hearts of all the spectators with great awe, — that the Virgin Mary is sometimes represented in Greek art with three hands.

Another council soon restored the pictures of the Virgin to their former places in churches, where they have been seen ever since. But most of these images are to be found in the Roman, Greek, Syrian, Coptic, Abyssinian, and Armenian churches, where she is viewed with particular veneration.

From the East, the worship of the Virgin soon extended to the West, where she was already very popular in the days of Charlemagne. It was then that returning pilgrims brought back fragments of the apocryphal gospels, which, owing to the prevailing ignorance, were believed implicitly, although the fathers of the Church had already declared them unworthy of a place in the canon.

At the time of the Crusades, the worship of the Virgin received a new impetus; and it is then that the title Our Lady or Madonna came into general use. Hundreds of knights, starting out for the Holy Land, pledged themselves to Mary's service, wore her image or colours as a token, and used her name as watchword and battle-cry. The monks, equally eager to show their devotion, wore white in memory of her purity, black in respect for her sorrows; and each order became the champion of some doctrine concerning her, such as the Immaculate Conception, for instance, which was supported by the Franciscans in particular.

Those were the days of visions, too, and Saint Bernard relates that he once saw two ladders leading up to heaven. At the head of one of them stood the Lord Jesus, at the top of the other His Virgin mother. Both gazed with benevolent eyes upon the sinners painfully climbing upward to the heavenly heights; but while Christ remained motionless, Mary stretched out her hands to help the strugglers surmount the last obstacles, and tenderly drew them up into heaven. This vision, which, he explained, showed the Virgin as taking pity upon and helping sinful mortals, of course served to strengthen the faithful in their allegiance to the Queen of Heaven.

The time of the Crusades was also a period of intense devotion, and the painters of images, who were at that time mostly monks, often went to their work after spending hours in penance and prayer, and in some cases painted Christ and the Virgin only upon their knees.

The returning crusaders and pilgrims related the tales they had heard in the East; and the minstrels wandered from door to door, reciting stories and singing ballads on sacred subjects which were popular everywhere.

It is thus that the apocryphal traditions became generally known, even before the Church began to make use of series of pictures for the instruction and edification of the faithful. It was then, too, that the religious plays, which first formed part of the Mass, were given outside of the churches, and in a far different way.

It had long been customary to have a sort of representation of the descent of the angel Gabriel at the feast of the Annunciation. Then came the exhibition of the Nativity at Christmas, the procession of the Magi at Epiphany, the altar strewn with white flowers at the Purification, the burial of the Cross on Good Friday, and its restoration on the altar on Easter, in memory of the glorious Resurrection of Our Lord. The next step in dramatic performances had been the Passion Play attributed to Gregory

Nazianzen. This was followed by countless similar plays, and as it became finally customary to exhibit the mocking of Christ, on or about the first of April, the Passion d'Avril became by corruption the " Poisson d'Avril," or the popular expression for " April fool " in France.

When the plays were no longer seen in the churches, the monks ceased to serve as actors, and the dramatic performances were given either by the guilds of the large cities, or by strolling bands of performers, the most celebrated being the French Confrérie de la Passion. The great centres for these plays in England were Coventry and Chester, where the guilds gave elaborate representations, which were kept up until the days of Shakespeare.

In course of time the religious purpose was almost lost sight of, and the amusement of the public was considered rather than their edification and instruction. To introduce a comic element, the shepherds camping out on the hillside on Christmas eve played all manner of tricks upon one another, demons took the place of clowns, and Herod was made to rant upon the stage, until he became a fit subject for the proverb to out-Herod Herod, which we owe to Shakespeare.

The stage, in England, was generally placed

on wheels, and these huge carts were dragged from place to place for the performance of the plays. As in some cases the actors played their parts both on the stage and in the street, they frequently took advantage of the latter circumstance to indulge in side play with the spectators; and this always proved a very popular feature of the entertainment.

The scenery was, of course, of the most primitive description, but the costumes were very gorgeous if not strictly correct. God the Father wore a gold wig to distinguish Him from the other actors; and the angels were gilded, until it was discovered that this process was injurious to the health of those representing them. Old account-books throw strange lights upon these performances, which, beginning with the Downfall of Satan and the Creation of the World, concluded only with the Last Judgment. Among other strange items, we find:—

> " Paid to the players for rehearsal,
> Imprimis to God ii *s.* viii *d.*
> Item to Pilate his wife, ii *s.*
> Paid to Fauston for cock crowing, iii *d.*
> Paid for mending Hell, ii *d.*
> Paid for painting of Hell mouth, iii *d.*
> Item for setting World on Fire, v *d.*"

Of all these plays, only one has survived, and is still given every ten years. This is the Passion Play of Ober-Ammergau, which has been remodelled and expurgated, until it is now one of the most impressive dramatic representations in the world. Like the early plays, it is used as a means of revival, and the actors who participate in its production are animated by the most reverent feelings.

The general worship of the Virgin, and especially the disputes concerning the Immaculate Conception, attracted the public attention to Mary's parents, who were duly canonised. Joseph, too, was admitted to the rank of saint, and others soon followed, until the Church calendar became quite full. With the invention of printing, a new stimulus was given to learning; and one of the first books sent out from the press was a poem by Gerson, where not only the Virgin Mary, but Joseph, Anna, and Joachim, were all recommended to the veneration of the faithful. Then too, with the Renaissance, came the great revival of classical art and literature, which exerted such an influence that the pictures and statues, from merely conventional, gradually became natural and beautiful.

It was at about this epoch that artists began to represent the Holy Family, introducing into the picture not only the Virgin and Child, but Joseph, Joachim, Anna, Zacharias, Elizabeth, and the infant Saint John. For a time now, the outward form rather than the religious idea became paramount; and instead of painting upon their knees, like some of their predecessors, a few of the artists used notoriously bad women for models, and set up these pictures to be worshipped in the churches.

This state of affairs was, of course, very distasteful to the truly religious; and Savonarola, among others, protested vehemently against these effigies, some of which he publicly burned. These denunciations were not without effect; and painters again sought to represent the Virgin, not only as the most beautiful woman whom their fancy could suggest, but also as the purest and best. To express the combination of human and divine in her nature, to remind the spectator of her mission upon earth, to recall special events in her history, the artists now placed around her many symbols. As their meaning is not always obvious, we will explain a few of them here, referring the reader to art histories for a more detailed list.

The sun, moon, and stars are often introduced, in allusion to the vision of Saint John, as recorded

PREDESTINATION OF THE VIRGIN. (MÜLLER.)

in the Apocalypse. Sometimes a star is embroidered on the Virgin's veil, or mantle, or forms a clasp for the latter garment; this is because one of the Hebrew meanings of her name is "Star of the Sea." When she wears a crown of twelve stars, or when twelve stars appear in any part of the picture, they are intended to represent either the twelve apostles, or the twelve tribes of Israel. The crescent moon and stars generally appear, together with many cherubim, in paintings called the Immaculate Conception.

> "The Virgin Mother stood,
> Down from her flowing hair to sandal-shoon,
> The mystic type of maiden motherhood.
> Below her feet there curved a crescent moon,
> And all the golden planets were her hood;
> In comely folds her queenly garb was moulded,
> And over her pure breast her hands were folded."
>
> ALFRED AUSTIN: *Madonna's Child*.[1]

Many pictures, where the sun forms the background, and where Mary is crowned with twelve stars, are also called the Immaculate Conception. But where her foot rests upon a dragon or serpent,— the emblem of Satan,— holding in one claw an apple,— the emblem of

[1] Macmillan & Co.

sin, — the picture should be called the Predestination of the Virgin; because it is intended to convey an idea of her mission upon earth, as announced to Adam and Eve in the Garden of Eden.

The lily is always a symbol of purity. In the Annunciation, the lily is generally without stamens; but when the picture sets forth Mary as the patron saint of France or of Florence, the stamens are not omitted. Thorns twined around lilies are in allusion to the Virgin's sorrows as well as to her purity. In allusion to the Scripture text, "I am the Rose of Sharon," roses are frequently introduced. They are also the emblems of love and beauty; and, besides the legends already given concerning them, Sir John Mandeville gives us the following quaint tale: —

Mary, "blamed with wrong and sclaundered with fornication, was demed to the Dethe, and as the Fyre beganne to brenne aboute hire, sche made hire Preyers to oure Lord, that as sche was not gylty of that Synne, that he wold helpe hire, and make it to be knowen to alle men, of his mercyfulle grace. And when sche hadde thus seyd, anon was the Fyer quenched and oute, and the Brondes that weren kyndled becomen red Roses, and the Brondes that weren not kyndled becomen white Roseres and fulle of Roses. And theise weren the first Roseres and Roses, bothe white and red that ever ony man saughe. And thus was this maiden saved by the Grace of God."

> "The stake
> Branches and buds, and spreading its green leaves,
> Embowers and canopies the fair maid,
> Who thus stands glorified; and Roses, then
> First seen on earth since Paradise was lost,
> Profusely blossom round her, white and red,
> In all their rich variety of hues."
> SOUTHEY.

Among other symbols we find, still in allusion to texts in the Old Testament, the Enclosed Garden, the Well, the Fountain, the Tower of David, the Temple of Solomon, the City of David, the Closed Gate, the Sealed Book, the Palm, and the Cedar, the Olive, and the Rod of Jesse, or flowering rod. All these symbols further serve as means to express some Biblical truth, or some quality, such as the indestructibility of the cedar, or the loftiness of the palm; while, as every one knows, the olive is the emblem of peace. Mary is often invoked by these and similar names, as well as represented with, or accompanied by, the symbols they indicate.

> "Tower of David, Ivory Tower,
>   Vessel of Honour, House of God,
>   Mystical Rose, unfading Flower,
>   Sure refuge of the unconsoled,
>   Pray for us!
>
> "Mirror of Justice, Wisdom's Seat,
>   Celestial shade for earthly heat,
>   The sinner's last and best retreat
>   Pray for us! Pray for us!"
>   ALFRED AUSTIN: *Madonna's Child*.[1]

The globe and sceptre are both emblems of sovereignty; the serpent is the type of Satan or sin; and an apple, the sign of the fall of man, which necessitated the coming of the Redeemer. Besides the flowers, we often see fruits or grain introduced: wheat is used to represent the bread of life, grapes are an allusion to the sacramental wine, and the pomegranate is the emblem of hope, on account of its red colour, the sign of the Cross perceived where it is cut, and the five seeds which serve to represent the five wounds of Christ.

> "All hath been told her touching her dear Son,
>   And all shall be accomplished: where He sits
>   Even now, a Babe, He holds the symbol fruit."
>   DANTE GABRIEL ROSSETTI.

[1] Macmillan & Co.

The dove, so often seen, represents the Holy Ghost, while seven doves typify the seven gifts of the Spirit. Birds are generally emblems of the soul, although the Goldfinch is rather a type of the Passion, which is signified by the blood-red marks upon its wings.

Besides being represented as already described in a previous chapter, the Annunciation is sometimes depicted by an allegory, which was popular in the Middle Ages. In such pictures the unicorn, an emblem of chastity, pierces the breast of the Virgin. The unicorn, wounding only to heal, typifies the Lord Jesus; while the four hounds in hot pursuit are personifications of mercy, truth, justice, and peace. The huntsman, holding the hounds in leash, or winding his horn, is meant to represent the angel Gabriel.

Old Testament figures are sometimes introduced to set forth its connection with events in the New; and thus, in paintings by the old masters, there are often several pictures combined into one not inharmonious whole. Because some of the old Greek pictures grew dark with age, and on account of the Scripture passage, " I am dark but comely," the Virgin is sometimes represented with a very swarthy complexion; and, strange to relate, such pictures are held in much greater veneration than any others.

In all historical works of art the Virgin Mary is very simply clad, a red tunic with long sleeves, an ample blue mantle, and a veil being the prescribed costume. But in devotional pictures, and particularly in those where she is called the Virgin Enthroned, or the Queen of Heaven, she is most gorgeously arrayed. In the Immaculate Conception, and in the Assumption, her tunic is pure white, or merely spangled with gold stars; but during the Passion Week, and after the Crucifixion, she is always represented as wearing violet or gray.

Until the fifteenth century, the Child was always clad in swaddling clothes, or short tunic; but after that period, it became customary to represent Him either partly or wholly undraped. The adult Christ is, however, always fully clad, and generally in a white and "seamless" robe. It is only in the Baptism in the Jordan, the Washing of the Disciples' Feet, the Flagellation, and the Crucifixion, that this long garment is removed.

As the pictures of the Virgin and Child are far too numerous to count, and as one artist has frequently painted a score of pictures which are called by the same title, most of the Madon-

MADONNA DI SAN SISTO. (Raphael.)

nas are designated by some accessory which has been introduced. Hence, we hear of the Madonna of the Lily, and of the Madonna of the Goldfinch (Cardellino). When the picture stands in some conspicuous place, or was painted for some noted person, it is generally distinguished by such a title as the Sistine Madonna, because one of the kneeling figures is Pope Sextus II., or as Madonna del Gran Duca, because painted for the Grand Duke of Florence.

Besides the names which have already been given, the Virgin boasts of a few more connected with legends which have been the subject of pictures by well-known artists. Such is, for instance, the title of Our Lady of the Snow. It seems that a Roman Patrician, having no children to whom he might bequeath his great wealth, once prayed Mary to teach him how best to dispose of it. His prayers ended, the Patrician fell asleep; and although it was in the month of August, 352, he dreamed that the Virgin appeared to him, and bade him build a church in her honour, in a place where he would find snow on the morrow.

When the Roman Patrician awoke, he related his dream to his wife. She too was deeply impressed by the vision which he had had; and they both went in search of the Pope, carrying with them the plan of a church such as the Patrician had seen in his dream.

The Roman and his wife knelt at the Pope's feet, besought his permission to build a church in honour of the Virgin, and related the vision which had prompted this pious thought. The tale they told so aroused the Pope's interest, that he and his clergy went out with them, and, in spite of the intense heat of a Roman summer, they found a freshly fallen patch of snow upon the Esquiline hill. Here the Patrician built a church, which is known as Santa Maria Maggiore; and ever since then Mary has added the title of Our Lady of the Snow to those which she already possessed. The Patrician's Dream is the subject of several noted pictures, in one of which, by Murillo, he and his wife are lost in peaceful slumber while the Virgin hovers over them, and in one corner of the painting are the plans of the future church. In a companion picture, the Patrician and his wife are kneeling before the Pope explaining their wishes to him, while in the background an ecclesiastical procession is seen going toward Mount Esquiline.

Mary is also called Our Lady of Loretto, because it is claimed that the house where she was born, and where the Annunciation took place, was miraculously transported from Nazareth to Loretto, in Italy. It seems that the Saracens once threatened to profane this building, and that four angels, seizing it by the corners, wafted it speedily over land and sea. They set their precious burden down in Dalmatia; but as the people there were not worthy to have it remain amongst them, the angels again took it up and bore it over the Adriatic to Loretto, where it has been the object of pious veneration ever since 1295. The Santa Casa, as Mary's house is called, has since then been entirely covered with white marble, exquisitely sculptured by eminent artists. Some of these bas-reliefs represent the translation of the House of Mary. Our Lady of Loretto is sometimes depicted as seated on the roof of the house, while it is borne aloft by the angels, and calmly nursing the Christ Child, whom she holds in her arms.

According to a Spanish legend, the Apostle Saint James, while preaching the Gospel in Spain, was once favoured by a strange vision. He saw the skies open, and an alabaster pillar descend to earth. There, seated on the top of the pillar, he beheld the Virgin Mary holding her Babe. This vision soon vanished; but a church was built upon the spot where the pillar rested, and Our Lady of the Pillar is considered the special protectress of Saragossa, the place where this miracle occurred.

If we were to attempt to relate here all the miracles which are said to have taken place in connection with many of the Madonna pictures, it would require far more space than is usually allowed for one book. Besides, they are recorded in many of the guide-books, and have no interest except for people who visit the place where the miracle is said to have happened.

But the legends of the painters, and of the circumstances under which some noted pictures were painted, are of great interest. The most charming of them all, however, is the one connected with Raphael's Madonna della Sedia, or Our Lady of the Chair.

An old hermit, Father Bernardo, had built a little retreat for himself in the Italian hills. He was a very good man, and spent so much time in meditation and prayer that the neighbouring people all honoured him as a saint, and often came to him for advice. In visiting him, they often asked how he could endure such a life, and whether he did not feel very lonely at times?

The old man would shake his head, smile gently, and tell them that although solitude had no terrors for him, he could, whenever he pleased, enjoy the society of his two daughters, one of whom was talkative, while the other was silent. The people were at first greatly mystified by this answer; but they finally discovered that the old man was alluding to Mary, the daughter of a neighbouring vine-dresser, whom he had known from a child, and carefully taught, while his second daughter was the huge oak beneath which he had built his hermitage.

Time passed on, and one spring there was a terrible storm in the hills. The mountain streams became torrents, and the freshet swept away houses and cattle. When the people had managed to recover from their first terror, they immediately thought of the poor old hermit, whose hut lay so near the mountain stream that they felt sure it must have been swept away.

They were all convinced that the hermit had perished; but Mary, the vine-dresser's daughter, prayed that her good old master might be safe. As soon as the storm abated, she took some provisions, and, in spite of the danger, went in search of the hermit. When she came near the place where his hut had stood, she uttered a cry of terror, for no trace of it remained, and only the oak stood erect.

Her cry was, however, immediately answered by another, and, gazing in the direction whence it proceeded, Mary saw the hermit, clinging to the branches of the oak, but almost fainting from exhaustion. By her efforts, the old man was soon rescued from his perilous position; and after he had returned thanks to God for his marvellous escape, he turned to the people and said: "I owe my preservation to my two daughters, as well as to God, and I hope He will reward them both by distinguishing them in some way from the other works of His hand."

Some time after this the old monk died. Mary married a cooper; and the oak, cast down by another storm, was hewn into pieces and used to make the staves and heads of wine-casks.

Raphael, the painter, was at that time wandering on foot through the country, accompanied by a few of his pupils to whom he pointed out the beauties of nature. He had long been searching for a suitable model for a new Madonna, which he had been commissioned to paint. In the course of his wanderings, he came at last to the secluded valley, where the cooper was merrily hammering his casks. Mary, his wife, sat in a chair, on the porch of his little vine-grown cottage, tenderly nursing her second child, while the eldest played with some sticks by her side. The child had just fastened two of the twigs together, in the shape of a cross, and was lean-

MADONNA DELLA SEDIA. (Raphael.)

ing against his mother's knee, to show it to her, when the painter came upon the scene.

At the very first glance Raphael perceived the beauty and touching grace of the picture, and exclaiming that here was the model he had sought so long in vain, he glanced eagerly around him for sketching materials. As there was neither canvas nor paper at hand, he drew a sketch of the picture on the smooth head of a cask which the cooper was just finishing.

Raphael's pupils, and the honest workman, gazed at him in admiration, as he rapidly sketched the tender mother, and both her little children. When the sketch was finished, Raphael paid the cooper liberally for the barrel-head, which he carried away with him. As soon as he arrived home, he finished the picture on the wood upon which he sketched it, and thus the old monk's prayer was granted. Mary had sat as model for one of the loveliest Virgins the world has ever seen, and her beauty was made well-nigh indestructible by the solidity of the oaken board upon which it was painted, and which came from the very heart of the old monk's favourite tree.

It is a great pity to spoil this legend by confessing that the Madonna della Sedia is painted upon canvas, and not upon wood. The shape of the picture however is exactly that of the head of a wine-cask, and as a round picture was very rare at that time, it bears out the story, which, if not true, is at least, as the Italians say, "ben trovata," or happily imagined.

Besides historical series of pictures, setting forth the lives of Christ and the Virgin Mary, we have others, which are most frequently seen in the Roman Catholic Churches. Thus, we find a series of five pictures called the Joyful Mysteries, and representing the Annunciation, the Visitation, the Nativity, the Purification, and Mary finding the twelve-year-old Christ in the Temple.

Next come the Five Dolorous Mysteries, which include Christ in the Garden of Gethsemane, the Flagellation, the Crown of Thorns, the Procession to Calvary, and the Crucifixion with Mary at the foot of the Cross.

The Five Glorious Mysteries are the Resurrection, the Ascension, the Descent of the Holy Ghost, the Assumption, and the Coronation of the Blessed Virgin Mary.

At times, some of these pictures, together with others, are formed into groups of seven subjects. Then we have the Seven Joys of the Virgin Mary, *i. e.*, the Annunciation, the Visitation, the Adoration of the Magi, the Presentation of the Christ-Child in the Temple, the Finding of the twelve-year-old Jesus, the Assumption, and the Coronation.

The companion series is called the Seven Sorrows of the Virgin Mary, and sets forth the Prophecy of Simeon, the Flight, the Loss of the twelve-year-old Jesus, the Betrayal of Christ, the Crucifixion, the Descent from the Cross, and the Ascension with Mary left on earth and longing for her vanished Son.

Another very well-known series of pictures is called the Stations of the Holy Way of the Cross. These pictures are generally placed all around the church. The series begins at the High Altar. We have : 1, Jesus Condemned to Death ; 2, Jesus made to bear His Cross ; 3, Jesus' first fall beneath the burden of the Cross ; 4, Jesus meets His afflicted Mother ; 5, the Cyrenean helps Jesus to carry His Cross ; 6, Veronica wipes the face of Jesus ; 7, Jesus' second fall beneath the weight of the Cross ; 8, Jesus speaks to the daughters of Jerusalem ; 9, Jesus' third fall ; 10, Jesus stripped of His garments ; 11, Jesus nailed to the Cross ; 12, Jesus dies on the Cross ; 13, Jesus taken down from the Cross ; 14, Jesus laid in the Sepulchre.

There are a few more styles of pictures which are designated by particular terms, such as the

Incoronata, or Crowned Virgin, the type of the Church Triumphant; the Virgin of Mercy, or the Intercessor; the Mater Dolorosa, or the Mother mourning for her suffering or dead Son. In this last-named character, the Virgin Mary is sometimes also called the Queen of Martyrs, because her sufferings surpassed those of any of the Christians who died to testify their belief in her Son. The Stabat Mater is the Virgin standing at the foot of the Cross, watching the suffering which all her love cannot relieve even for a moment.

> "By the Cross, sad Vigil keeping,
> Stood the mournful mother weeping,
> While on it the Saviour hung;
> In that hour of deep distress,
> Pierced the sword of bitterness,
> Through her heart, with sorrow wrung."
>
> *Stabat Mater Dolorosa.*

La Pietà, is the Virgin holding her dead Son in her arms, on her knees, or bending over Him as He lies at her feet. There are besides these many devotional representations of the Madonna, especially votive pictures, where the Virgin, enthroned, is surrounded sometimes by angels and saints, and where the family or individual for whom the picture was painted, in fulfilment of a solemn vow, is often seen kneeling in the foreground.

The most pleasing of all the representations of the Virgin is that called the Mater Amabilis. Here she is no longer an object of worship, but merely the tender mother bending over her Child.

> "'The mother with the Child
> Whose tender winning arts,
> Have to His little arms beguiled
> So many wounded hearts."
>
> M. ARNOLD.

As we have seen, the legends of Christ and the Virgin Mary have had great influence over art and literature. They are also closely connected with botany, and it is said that the " Life of Christ flings its shadow over the whole vegetable world."

Many plants, besides those already mentioned, are closely bound to religious tradition, — such as the Vervain or Verbena, which is popularly known as the Holy Herb. It is supposed that this plant sprouted in the Garden of Gethsemane, from the bloody drops of perspiration which fell from Our Lord's brow. This herb is therefore credited with marvellous healing properties, and used to be gathered with special reverence.

"Hail to thee, Holy Herb,
Growing on the ground,
On the Mount of Olivet
First wert thou found.

"Thou art good for many an ill,
And healest many a wound;
In the name of sweet Jesus
I lift thee from the ground."

DYER: *Folk Lore of Plants*.[1]

Next comes the Blessed Herb, with trefoil leaf, an emblem of the Trinity, and blossoms with five golden petals, which stand for the five wounds of Christ. There is besides, as it were, a whole botanical calendar, for we are told that the stars of Bethlehem bloomed at the Nativity, and that the snowdrops opened when Our Saviour was carried into the Temple, and are hence considered particularly appropriate for church decoration at the Feast of the Purification.

The red spots on Saint-John's-wort are said to appear on the anniversary of the day on which he was beheaded, and the arum persicaria has the same spots because it grew at the foot of the Cross.

A number of the botanical legends are closely

---

[1] Appleton & Co.

connected with the Cross itself. For instance, we are told that Mary, on her way to Jerusalem with the Infant Christ, sat down under a fig-tree by the wayside to nurse Him. As she was resting there, a sudden shivering fit seized her, and a presentiment of coming sorrow made her clasp her Child closer to her heart. Although Mary did not know it, it seems that this tree was the same which Christ cursed on account of its barrenness so many years later. Some authorities claim that Judas hanged himself on this withered fig-tree; but others assert that the executioners found it when seeking wood for the Redeemer's Cross, and that they hewed it down for that express purpose.

The Cross is also said to have been made from the mistletoe, which used to be a large tree, but which, thus incurring a curse, was dwarfed and reduced to the mean proportions of a parasite. This same reason is given for the stunted proportions of the dwarf birch, and sundry other species of trees which do not attain their full growth.

The trembling which agitates the leaves of certain trees, and particularly of the poplar and the aspen, is, as we have already seen, ascribed to the horror felt by the wood, when called upon to bear the dying Saviour.

Some writers claim that the Cross was made of four kinds of wood, the emblems of the four points of the compass. These species vary, however, and are either the cedar, cypress, palm, and olive, or the cedar, cypress, pine, and box.

"Nailed were His feet to Cedar, to Palm His hands,
Cypress His body bore, title on Olive stands."

Another legend claims that when the men went out in search of wood, that all the trees split rather than become accomplices to the death of Our Lord, and that the Oak alone remained whole. But this story does not hinder the inhabitants of various parts of the world from claiming that the Cross was made of ash or elder, or of any other tree which strikes their fancy as appropriate.

Many flowers and fruits are said to bear the imprint of the Cross, which can be found in the centre of the red poppy, in the gourd, and in the banana, which the inhabitants of the Canary Islands never cut with a knife, on that account.

When the Spaniards came into South America, and first beheld the Passion Flower, they cried aloud that Christ had laid His seal upon the land, by causing such a marvellous flower to grow and publish there His death on the Cross.

The five anthers of this blossom are said to represent the five wounds of Our Lord; the triple style, the three nails; the pistil, the pillar to which the Saviour was bound; the filaments, the crown of thorns; and the calyx, the nimbus, or glory around Him.

> " The Passion-flower long has blow'd
> To betoken us sign of the Holy Rood."

All the white flowers are dedicated to the Virgin Mary, and during her month — May — the altars in the Roman Catholic churches are adorned by a profusion of pure white blossoms. Many other blossoms also bear her name. One species of Orchid is called Our Lady's Slipper; the common ribbon grass, Our Lady's Garter; the dodder, Our Lady's Laces; the marigold, Our Lady's Smock; the maiden's-hair fern is also known as Our Lady's Tresses.

An experienced botanist, the Rev. Hilderic Friend, has given a very complete and whimsical description of the plants connected with Mary which we cannot refrain from quoting here: " How liberal we have been toward her ladyship will appear when I enumerate some of the plants with which she is honoured. Thus, as she reclines in her bower we provide her with boots and slippers for her feet, garters with which to keep her hose in place, and laces for her corset or shoes. We have found her a thimble and needle with which to sew, a smock and a mantle in which to garb herself, a cushion on which to recline, and a comb and a looking-glass for her hair and tresses which we also have supplied her. Thus equipped, we find her a nightcap to keep her curls from being ruffled at night, and, when she needs to write to her friends, we find her a seal or a signet for her letter. She would be incomplete without fingers, and these we also provide, together with a navel, and a basin in which to wash. And, having done all this, we plant around her bower, trees, grass, whin, clover, cowslip, mint, bracken, foxglove, fern, and thistle to make the garden gay. We further find her in gloves for her delicate fingers, eardrops to adorn her head, and a riband with which to tie back her hair or make up a sash. She is not content without ruffles, and these too are found for her, and lest she should lose her money, a purse is also provided; yet, with all this lavish kindness, we make her sleep on a bed of straw."

Many artists, conversant with the popular superstitions about plants, place in the foreground of their pictures, herbs and flowers which have a particular message for those who can read their hidden meaning. It is thus that every detail, even the most insignificant, often has some special purpose.

Our aim in this volume has been to explain some of these meanings, so that those who have not studied the matter, and are not artists, can nevertheless understand the most important stories told by the pictures they see. It is a fascinating occupation to trace out every allusion for one's self; but unless a large collection of pictures is available, a long list of paintings where the various symbols can be seen is aggravating to the average reader.

Only a few paintings have therefore been mentioned here, and those are so well known, owing to the manifold reproductions of them, that all can recall them without any effort. It is only when the *story* is clearly understood that the finer and often hidden meaning of the artist can be seen, and that we can best perceive the many lessons besides those of faith, hope, and charity which are taught by most of the pictures of the Virgin and of Christ.

THE END.

www.ingramcontent.com/pod-product-compliance
Lightning Source LLC
Chambersburg PA
CBHW032048220426
43664CB00008B/917